Living in an Icon

A Program for Growing Closer to Creation and to God

Robert Gottfried &
Frederick W. Krueger

CHURCH
PUBLISHING
INCORPORATED

Church Publishing
19 East 34th Street
New York, NY 10016
www.churchpublishing.org

Cover design: Jennifer Kopec, 2 Pug Design
Interior design and layout: Beth Oberholtzer Design

A record of this book is available from the Library of Congress.

ISBN-13: 9781640652361 (pbk.)
ISBN-13: 9781640652378 (ebook)

The whole earth is a living icon of the face of God.
—St. John of Damascus (675-749)
(aggregate of a paragraph*)

The glory of God is the human fully alive.
—St. Irenaeus (c. 202 CE)

*On the Divine Images, trans. David Anderson (New York: St Vladimir's Seminary Press, 1980), 23–25. Aggregate of the entire paragraph.

Contents

Introduction

You are about to embark on a great adventure. This adventure will take you to the "Great Out-Of-Doors" and the "Great Indoors," the great worlds about and within you. As such, it will challenge every part of your being and may turn out to be one of the most exciting and fulfilling enterprises you will ever undertake.

Living in an Icon attempts to bring us back in touch with all of God's creation and with God's presence in the world. In the Orthodox world, icons serve as portals through which a believer can encounter God. God's presence shines through the painting. As St. John of Damascus said, "The whole earth is a living icon, a portal through which we encounter God's presence."[1] As we will see, growing closer to God involves growing closer to God's creation. Similarly, truly getting to know creation involves growing closer to God and getting to know what lies deep within it. If we can develop "ears that hear and eyes that see" (Prov. 20:12, NIV), our whole life can become a prayer. *Living in an Icon* builds on this simple beginning and helps us learn to pray without ceasing, to live in such a way that all the world reveals God's presence to us.

While much of what we will be doing in *Living in an Icon* is building a prayer-filled life, this program differs in its focus and purpose from programs such as centering prayer that instruct participants in how to pray. Rather, our aim here is to help one another grow in such a way that all of one's daily life is a prayer, so that we "pray constantly" as St. Paul encourages us. This, of course, is the goal of monastic communities. Accordingly, we

---

1. *On the Divine Images,* trans. David Anderson (New York: St. Vladimir's Seminary Press, 1980), 23–25. Aggregate of the entire paragraph.

utilize a few aspects of monastic formation in our program, particularly drawing on the Benedictine approach to growing closer to God. What we are presenting here is as old as the church. We have just repackaged some portions in a modern setting.

Typical monastic formation involves 1) development of attitudes and ways of life that are conducive to spiritual growth, 2) communal life that reinforces and informs that growth, and 3) prayer. Our program has elements of all three. Thus, we can think of *Living in an Icon* as a program of spiritual growth, of developing a spiritual life in the contemplative tradition. So while *Living in an Icon* is all about prayer, it's not about deepening one's ability to pray using any particular form or practice.

This program assumes you already have established some sort of prayer life, such as centering prayer, reading prayers from a book, or reflecting on scripture. We have included a discussion of prayer in Appendix 2 in case you have not. Appendix 3 offers additional resources on prayer. Even if you do have an established prayer life, you may find these useful.

Meditation and Contemplation in *Living in an Icon*

Living in an Icon focuses on two types of prayer: meditation and contemplation. In Christianity, meditation equates to reflecting on a "text," whether it be a passage in a book or a tree in the forest. We think about what we have seen, asking what it tells us about ourselves, life, and God. When we contemplate, however, we attempt to come before God in silence, seeking to encounter God directly without words.

Monastic tradition holds that if one eventually wants to attain a sense of oneness with God, what they call the mystic experience, the seeker needs to grow in two ways. First, they need to develop attitudes and approaches to life that bring them more in line with God's own character. This personal growth and development takes time. Second, they must spend time contemplating nature, learning to encounter God in the works of God's hands. *Living in an Icon* focuses initially on building the attitudes and behaviors that facilitate meditation and, ultimately, contemplation. Thus, it moves from an emphasis on reflection and active engaging with the world through the senses to silence and a deeper relationship with all creation, and finally to deeper encounters with God through nature. It does this by repeatedly going into the natural world and then applying what one learns there to the world of everyday life.

Consequently, we have divided the program into three segments, or "journeys," that reflect this progression: Waking Up, The Road to Kinship, and Encountering the Burning Bush. Providing three shorter modules offers you flexibility in how you use this material. You can read about this below.

The Book of Nature and Travel Abroad

The ancient church fathers (and many who have followed in their footsteps) said that all of creation was a book, the "Book of Nature," which stood in equal importance with the "Book of Scripture" because in each case God wrote the words. After all, God spoke creation into being. Each creature and rock constitute an individual word of the book, one of the many *logoi* spoken by the *Logos*, or Word of God. Without creation the early fathers said we would misunderstand scripture, and without scripture, we would misunderstand creation.

Accordingly, St. Augustine (354–430), the great theologian, would declare:

> Some people, in order to discover God, read books. But there is a great book: the very appearance of created things. Look above you! Look below you! Note it. Read it. God whom you want to discover, never wrote that book with ink. Instead He set before our eyes the things that He had made. Can you ask for a louder voice than that? Why, heaven and earth shout to you: "God made me!"[2]

---

2. Vernon J. Bourke, trans. and ed., *The Essential Augustine* (Indianapolis: Hackett, 1974), 123. The text is from Sermon 126.6 in the Angelo Mai collection of Augustine's sermons, *Miscellanea Agustiniana,* ed. G. Morin (Rome, 1930), 1:355–68.

Or St. Bonaventure (1217–1274), a Franciscan, would proclaim:

Throughout the entire creation, the wisdom of God shines forth from Him and in Him, as in a mirror containing the beauty of all forms and lights and as in a book in which all things are written according to the deep secrets of God. . . . Truly, whoever reads this book will find life and will draw salvation from the Lord.[3]

Similarly, Martin Luther (1543–1846), the reformer, stated:

God writes the Gospel, not in the Bible alone, but also on trees, and in the flowers and clouds and stars.[4]

Many of us encounter God in the out-of-doors. Our experiences resonate with what our spiritual forefathers and mothers tell us. God speaks to us easily there. For us, therefore, nature and our everyday surroundings will serve as our monastery. They will teach us and form us if we allow the Holy Spirit to guide us in that process.

Spending quiet time in nature serves much the same function as travel or study abroad. When we travel abroad and experience a new culture, it gives us insight into the world that we left. In visiting Guatemala, for instance, we get a different perspective on life in the United States or wherever we live. We talk to new people, see new places, experience new ways of life. When we reflect on our experiences there, we find that we have new insights into the life back home. The natural world differs so much from everyday human experience that it serves just such a function. What we learn in nature yields new perspectives on everyday life, insights we might not gain otherwise. Thus, spending time in nature puts us in a place where we more easily can hear God speaking God's words to us.

---

3. *The Tree of Life (L'Arbre de Vie)* 12.46, Classics of Western Spirituality, trans. and ed. Ewert Cousins (New York: Paulist Press, 1978), 170.

4. Quoted in Caesar Johnson, ed., *To See a World in a Grain of Sand* (Norwalk, CT: C. R. Gibson, 1972), 24.

Accordingly, we will begin our journey by learning lessons from the Book of Nature, which we then can apply to our everyday life. We will begin our study abroad outside, moving back and forth from the Book of Nature to the book of everyday life. This way we will practice encountering God and responding to God wherever God may be, which is everywhere.

What This Asks of Us

What will all this require? First of all, it will require us to spend time outside. Ideally this would be around an hour a week in one "sitting." In our busy lives this can be difficult to do. If so, try two or three sessions of twenty or thirty minutes. However, if you really want to grow, then you need to dedicate time to the effort. This means making *Living in an Icon* a priority in your life. Just as getting physically fit requires discipline and effort, so does our spiritual life.

Second, sharing one's experiences with other people provides us the opportunity to learn from others and to gain perspective on our own experiences. Ideally, therefore, you would enter this process as part of a group, which would give you support and feedback as you continue on this journey. However, if you don't have a group, seek someone with whom you can share your insights and your struggles once a week or every other week. This person also can pray for you as well as you for them. Perhaps they would be willing to follow in the program with you. Having someone to whom you are accountable helps you keep going when time demands and other pressures start to mount up. So we highly recommend that you at least have one person with whom you can check in periodically.

Finally, you need a willingness to reflect on your experiences with the intention of learning from them and then changing as a result.

As we become more and more in line with the person God has called us to be, as we become more and more transparent so that God shines through us, we will find that all of creation, human and nonhuman, becomes a book that speaks to us. Similarly, if we listen to what creation speaks to us and respond appropriately, we will grow more and more into that person God always has intended us to be.

How to Use This Book

With the exception of the first and last chapters, each chapter contains an exercise or practice that you first will try out-of-doors and then apply during the week. Think of a place (or places) as natural as possible where you can take an hour or so each week to try a chapter's exercise for the first time. It could be a park or your backyard; if you live in the city far from a park, just a few potted plants. You don't have to go to the same place every time. In general, the more natural the area, the less human distractions you will find there.

The Taking It Home section at the end of each chapter instructs you on how to apply this practice throughout the next week or two until you move on to the next chapter (see the next paragraph). This way you allow God to teach you in nature (your study abroad experience) and then help you practice it in your daily life. If you persevere in your efforts, you will find that your experience in nature builds on your experience "at home" and vice versa. As you apply what you have learned in a variety of contexts, you will get better and better at it. This is a process you will continue for the rest of your life, for we never can truly master these exercises—we only can keep growing. No matter how tall we become, we never reach the sky. . . .

You will also want to have a journal or notebook in which you can jot down your reflections, experiences, or thoughts that come to you as you practice each exercise.

A short Note follows some chapters. These notes contain material that is important but that does not fit easily in the context of a chapter. They build on the material of the previous chapter, so read them sometime before beginning the next.

Taking the Program as Part of a Group

If you are using this book with a group, your facilitator will help guide you along the path and set the pace for the course. Each session may take from one to three weeks. The facilitator is there to guide group interactions more than to teach. You can expect to learn a great deal from other participants' experiences. The facilitator's role is to help you do so. If you want to facilitate a group, then please consult the *Living in an Icon: Facilitators Guide* (sold separately) for guidance.

Doing the Program on Your Own

Living in an Icon is best experienced as part of a group. However, if you are using this book on your own, then start with chapter 1: Reorientation. You can practice reorientation a few times before you choose to start on the first outdoor exercise, chapter 2: Noticing. Or you can try reorientation for the first time and then go right onto noticing. Then take each subsequent session/chapter at your own speed. When you feel you've gotten a reasonable handle on a practice, then move on to the next. It often takes at least three weeks of practicing any new thing for it to become a habit, so you may find it takes you that long to feel like you've really established a practice. However, if you already have been working on a certain practice before starting this book, you may find you can move more quickly on to the next one.

Ask the Spirit when to move on to the next chapter. Be aware of how you're reacting to a exercise. If you find you are resisting practicing it, ask yourself why and then try to address what you have learned. If your resistance really is getting in your way, then consider moving on to the next chapter with the option of going back and trying it again at a later date. The chapters build on one another, so we suggest taking them in the order given unless you have a particular reason for doing otherwise. You may find the Facilitator Guide that accompanies this text a useful resource in this process. In a sense, you are having to serve as your own facilitator. For that reason, you may find it useful to consult it for assistance in how best to proceed.

Given the difficulties of contemplating outdoors in cold weather and of finding time during Christmas holidays and vacations, you may choose to take each journey when you best can devote attention to it. In between each journey you can practice what you have learned up to that point. You profitably can revisit each module many times inasmuch as it takes more than a lifetime to master what each contains. So taking the three journeys with time in between is not a problem. Rather, having three journeys affords you the flexibility to adjust *Living in an Icon* to your personal circumstances and the opportunity to practice what you have learned before proceeding further, should you so choose.

Some Final Notes

Remember that you are developing a life of prayer. When you finish this book, you then will go on to practice what you have learned. You will never get too good at the practices of thanksgiving or beauty, for instance. You will find them infinitely enriching and worth returning to again and again. Also, you will find yourself constantly using the practices you have learned here in different combinations as you face different circumstances in your life. For awhile you may find that practicing hospitality, for example, helps you the most. Then you may find, when that doesn't seem to be doing the trick for you, that humility does. Similarly, since most practices involve aspects of the others, you may find that various combinations of them help you the most at different points in your life. In other words, you have developed a tool kit that you then can pick and choose from as the Holy Spirit guides you.

Finally, in the following pages when you encounter someone speaking in the first person, that is Robert (one of the authors) speaking. Now that we have covered all the introductory aspects of the program, let us begin.

JOURNEY
ONE

Waking Up

We might think of Journey One: Waking Up as beginning the process of truly learning to see. Every day presents us many opportunities to encounter and learn more about God, but all too often we fail to recognize them when they come our way. As Israel Baal Shem (c. 1698–1760) was said to have stated:

> The world is full of wonders and miracles but people take their little hands and cover their eyes and see nothing.[5]

The following six exercises in this first part of our journey encourage us to uncover our eyes, wake up from our existential naps, and engage with the world around us. In and of themselves they constitute some of the single most powerful exercises to help us along our path to growing in our ability to relate to both God and God's creation. George Washington Carver (1864–1943), the world-famous Tuskegee botanist, inventor, and modern Christian, had a prodigious ability to relate to plants and to God. He said that the key attitudes one needed in order to develop this ability consisted of loving plants, coming humbly before them, and experiencing awe and wonder in doing so.[6]

---

5. While Baal Shem Tov did not author anything, he is quoted saying this at http://www.livinglifefully.com/wonder.htm (accessed January 12, 2019).

6. Glenn Clark, *The Man Who Talks with the Flowers: The Life Story of Dr. George Washington Carver* (Shakopee, MN: Macalester Park, 1994), 39–43.

In journey one, we work on opening ourselves so that we might experience a deep wonder that far surpasses curiosity (we will work on love and humility in later journeys). This process leads us to recognize the giver of these wonders and to thank their creator for them. Many spiritual adepts, and increasingly many scientists, encourage us to develop an attitude of thanksgiving because of its power in bringing us closer to God and in improving our mental, physical, and emotional health. Journey one, then, ends on a high note.

CHAPTER 1
Reorientation

Besides this you know the time, that the hour has come
for you to wake from sleep. For salvation is nearer to us
now than when we first believed. (Rom. 13:11, ESV)

Sleeper, awake!
Rise from the dead,
and Christ will shine on you. (Eph. 5:14)

Rudolph Otto, a Lutheran theologian at the turn of the last century, produced a famous study[7] on the nature and cause of spiritual experiences. His study concluded that the lack of spiritual experience in many churchgoers is due to the busy pace of modern urban life, especially the lack of silence.

Jerry Mander, public relations and advertising executive, reports how researchers at Australian National University predicted that as television became more popular, there would be a corresponding increase in hyperactivity among children.[8] They correctly foresaw this effect because they saw television not as a teaching or entertainment vehicle so much as a mood alteration system, an external drug. The cumulative effect of the fast-paced electronic society, they concluded, "acts like a drug in the way it accelerates the human nervous system."[9] For those who are addicted to electronic media, it is harder to appreciate the wildness of nature because the natural world, in comparison, is a terrible slow-poke. To experience nature, to feel its subtleties, the human mind has to relax and slow down.

---

7. Rudolph Otto, *The Idea of the Holy: An Inquiry into the Non-Rational Factor in the Idea of the Divine and Its Relation to the Rational*, trans. John Harvey, 10th ed. (New York: Oxford University Press 1923, 1958).

8. Jerry Mander, *The Absence of the Sacred: The Failure of Technology and the Survival of the Indian Nations* (San Francisco: Sierra Club Book, 1991), 83–86.

9. Ibid., 84.

Thomas Merton (1915–1968) stated, "One has to be alone, under the sky before everything falls into place and one finds his own place in the midst of it all."[10] Then, he said that the doors of creation will open to you:

> When your tongue is silent, you can rest in the silence of the forest. When your imagination is silent, the forest speaks to you, tells you of its unreality and of the Reality of God. But when your mind is silent, then the forest suddenly becomes magnificently real and blazes transparently with the Reality of God.[11]

George Washington Carver said that people do not understand the spiritual lessons in creation because they are too preoccupied with the familiar and the comfortable so that they ignore what is spiritual and unfamiliar:

> Mysteries are things we don't understand because we have not learned to tune in. And finding true faith in the Creator is solving the greatest mystery of all.[12]

To illustrate this principle Carver told a story of how he once was invited to the home of a wealthy physician. Before they could speak, the host had to attend to some business. He invited George to go into the living room, turn on the radio, and listen to a concert playing on the radio. What happened though, said Carver, is that "I sat for an hour in silence. The music was there, but it was a mystery to me because I did not know how to turn on the radio and tune in the program."[13]

Each of these stories exemplifies some part of the modern predicament in learning from nature. Like for Carver, the lessons

---

10. Thomas Merton, *Conjectures of a Guilty Bystander* (Garden City, NY: Image Books [Doubleday], 1968), 294.

11. Thomas Merton, *Entering the Silence: Becoming a Monk & Writer,* The Journals of Thomas Merton (San Francisco: HarperSanFrancisco, 1995), 2:471.

12. Lawrence Elliott, *George Washington Carver: The Man Who Overcame* (New York: Prentice-Hall, 1966), 198.

13. Ibid., 198–99.

are there, but we do not know how to access them. So how do we learn to do so?

If we would "tune into" the lessons of nature, we must change our habitual approach to life. Slowing down, finding quiet, leaving behind the electronic pace of the media, getting exercise, moving out of our mental ruts—these are all starting points of reorientation.

The task of reorientation is simple: to connect to nature. To do so we have to connect at her speed. I can remember one of the first times I sat on somebody's front porch in the mountains of western North Carolina. I found the pace of the conversation excruciatingly slow. Long spaces of silence filled the time between our occasional observations on the day, how the same toad came hopping by at the same time day after day, or how the tobacco crop was faring. Over time, however, as I got in tune with my neighbors, I often found that the periods of silence were the times I cherished most deeply because we were comfortable with one another—we were "at home" in each other's presence. We communicated most when we didn't say a thing. Plants and animals take their good time to grow—my neighbors couldn't rush them and wouldn't gain a thing by rushing themselves (unless the hay needed to be harvested before it rained!). They took life at a measured pace that matched nature's rhythms.

For most of us today, however, our urban lives or our cybernetically connected occupations demand such a frenetic pace that it takes us time to slow down and adjust to the quiet pace of nature. We often live more in our thoughts than we do in the world we actually inhabit. We listen to our cellphones as we walk along instead of to the birds or the other sounds around us. We look down as we text our friends or colleagues instead of noticing the people and trees we are passing. We inhabit an electronic world of human making rather than the tangible physical world. Our own little worlds occupy our minds and hearts.

"We need to find God, and he cannot be found in noise and restlessness. God is the friend of silence," wrote Mother Teresa of Calcutta. "Trees, flowers, grass . . . grow in silence; see the stars, the moon and sun, how they move in silence."[14] In contrast, the clamor of cities, the hustle of highways, schedules and commitments, the din of the suburbs all make it hard to slow down—and so God seems far away.

To feel, we have to slow down. To relate meaningfully to other people, we must pay attention to them. Even to find time to read, we need to slow down. As a crucial step, we can try to leave the cares of the city behind and relax.

Reorientation is not a process that can be rushed or reduced to a precise formula. Each person is different. We each carry a unique set of concerns, concepts, tensions, and inhibitions. It takes time to relax, to let go of the hectic rush of the city, and to connect to the pace and peace of nature. Reorientation takes time because our mental activity carries a lot of inertia. Like a ship at sea, our habitual thought patterns do not change speed abruptly. We do not possess as much of a braking system as we might suppose. Instead, our mind gradually glides into a slower pace when we try to relax. Similarly, our attitudes, like paths across a meadow, resemble well-worn tracks and encrusted modes of travel. It requires great intentionality for us to change our attitudes and pace of life.

It's sometimes hard to remember that we, too, are animals, part of the created order. So we need to slow ourselves down to the pace of the rest of creation in order to relate to it. By doing so, not only do we get in touch with nature, but we get in touch with God.

So how can we slow down? One good way is to do something physical—dig in the garden, take a walk, do something with your hands. Exercising while focusing on the walking or how your body feels is another good way to get back in touch with your createdness. Just walking in the woods or down a road where you can look at the trees, or strolling through a park

---

14. Mother Teresa, "God is the Friend of Silence," in *A Treasury of Spiritual Wisdom*, ed. Andy Zubko (San Diego: Blue Dove Press, 1996), 429.

or garden, can reconnect us with the world around us. Nature itself has a way of helping us slow down and get back in touch.

However, just walking or working with our hands by itself won't necessarily get us in touch with God. We need intentionality about what we are doing. We always need to keep in mind that we are trying to establish a communion with the world around us and with God who moves through all things. In other words, there's a spiritual dimension to our slowing down and we need to keep that always firmly in our minds. We slow down not just to relax but to grow spiritually and to become whole.

So let's try an exercise we can use before we go out into nature or before we begin our workday. Over time when you go outside to contemplate, you may find that you often don't need to go through the reorientation process below. Even then, having some little ritual you always use can help you remember that you are setting this time aside in a special way. For some, this might consist of a psalm or a prayer that helps put you in touch with what you are about to do. Others might find it helpful to make a sign of the cross or to kneel and pray. The point is that we need something to help us realize that we are changing direction and are being intentional about what we are doing.

This reorientation exercise consists of three steps: 1) relaxing and quieting your mind until you are at peace with the world and yourself; 2) prayerfully lifting your mind, asking for the presence of Jesus Christ to fill you; 3) sitting in this presence for ten minutes. This exercise is both surprisingly easy but also deeply transforming. To make the steps even clearer, let me elaborate a bit on each:

1. Become quiet and relax.

- Find a quiet spot, either outside or inside. Sit down and become comfortable. Let go of all of your cares and especially of any animosities or anger or resentment. Relax.

- Take some deep breaths to flush out the thoughts and worries that have conditioned your thinking. You might find it helpful to inhale slowly for a count of six or eight and then slowly exhale through your lips for a count of eight. Having done this a few times, you might focus on how your breath feels as it passes in and out of your nasal passages and nose. Take your time. Let your body relax and sink into a rhythm of breathing.

- Become intentionally quiet. Commend yourself to God and surrender to the wisdom of the Creator's caring love.

2. Pray for the presence of Jesus Christ to fill you.

- Once you have quieted down, ask that the presence of Jesus Christ, his Holy Spirit, fill you.
- Continue in awareness of the life of Christ coming upon you. Continue to invoke His presence.

3. Sit still and enjoy the blessings of the Lord.

- Ask that the Holy Spirit overshadow your exercise and bring deep change to your thinking and insights. This will help you to become more receptive and alert to the lessons before and around you.
- Submit your life and your will to God. Relax in that "place."
- Conclude your exercise with thanks to God for God's presence now and at all times, and ask the Holy Spirit to guide you as you go out into creation, whether it be the woods or a city street.

Having done this, now go outside and take this stillness with you while you spend your hour or so outdoors. If you get distracted (as you probably will), perhaps starting to get restless, remind yourself that this is "time off" to spend with God and God's creation and reorient yourself to what you are doing. This is the first step at developing attentiveness and awareness, something we will be exploring a lot.

TAKING IT HOME

Try to spend a few minutes every day practicing reorientation. Just as we can reorient ourselves to opening ourselves to God's presence outdoors, we can do the same throughout our days of ordinary life. Particularly in an age of electronic distractions and the addiction they bring to constant input from media, developing an ability to tune them out and open oneself to God and to others presents a real challenge . . . and a marvelous opportunity. Like any skill, it also requires practice and dedication.

CHAPTER 2
Noticing

Learn how to look. Take time to look to see what's right there in front of you, to let what you see sink in. When you look at a flower opening or a tree moving with the wind, you just relax and take it all in. Try and see everything like that, if you can. —Robert Lax (1915–2000)[15]

If you're going to talk to God in nature, or experience nature speaking to you in some way, *you have to be aware that nature is there.* Or similarly, that God is there. This requires us to notice. Have you ever walked by somebody and not even realized that they are there? Or driven in the car awhile only to realize that you weren't aware that you had driven several miles? This is because you weren't awake. Much of our lives we live in a state of sleep. We're engaged in thinking, our minds deep in thought. So we pass through the world unaware of our surroundings.

If we are to encounter God in any context, we have to be alert for when God might be speaking to us or in any way trying to engage with us. If we want to communicate with God through nature, we have to be alert to the fact that nature is there. We can't just pass through it asleep. We have to wake up.

This exercise attempts to rouse us. After you have reoriented and prayed, just follow your nose. Spend an hour or so noticing the things about you. Look high, look low. Notice all the small things about your feet as well as the large views that you may encounter. You might find a magnifying glass useful to take with you. What do you smell? Hear? Taste? How do things feel?

---

15. John Dear, "The Wisdom of Robert Lax: 'Cultivate, Exercise Compassion,'" *National Catholic Reporter,* February 22, 2011, https://www.ncronline.org/blogs/road-peace/wisdom-robert-lax-cultivate-exercise-compassion.

Notice your reactions. How do you feel when you see something? Are you nervous? Tense? Peaceful? Joyful? Uneasy?

Choose a spot in nature that's nearby. It need not be particularly wild—it could be a cactus on your balcony. You don't have to go to the same place every time. In general, the more natural the area, the less human distractions you will find there and the easier this and the other exercises are to do.

While you are doing this and subsequent exercises, you may find that deep emotions emerge. That is a natural consequence of increasingly opening oneself up to God, oneself, and the world. For now, should that happen, be aware of those feelings. Acknowledge their presence. They are part of who you are at this moment, so respect their "right" to be there. Then, let them go—as they vie for your attention, don't dwell on them. Don't get distracted by trying to get rid of them. That just causes you to focus on them all the more. They are like a little child tugging at their parent's sleeve, asking for attention. If the parent says, "Now Freddie, I know that you want to talk, but Mommy is busy right now. Come back later and I'll spend time with you then," he often will go off satisfied and play by himself, knowing that he will get what he wants later. Do the same with strong feelings. Acknowledge grief, anger, or joy and then go on to the exercise again. Sometimes emotions are signs that we need to deal with something. Later on we will discuss how to approach resentments or hurts that come to light. For now, note your emotions' presence and return to noticing other things.

When you come back, take a few minutes to jot down what happened. *This needn't be burdensome*—even one or two sentences or just five descriptive words can suffice to jog your memory as to what transpired. Concentrate on your experiences. How did you feel when you saw something, heard something, smelled something? Try not to dwell on how you might interpret your experiences, but rather on what you noticed and how you reacted to them.

TAKING IT HOME

During the coming week, notice the things around you as you go about your daily life. Become aware of the people and the places you are passing, be aware of how you are feeling. Notice how your body feels. Are you tense or at ease? Do you feel rushed or frantic? Are you peaceful and collected? Do you find yourself thinking all the time, even when walking down the hall or talking with people? At the end of each day, you might find it helpful to jot down your reactions to what you've noticed during the day, just as you did outside. Again, write as much or as little as you wish. The idea is to provide something to help you remember your experiences. At the end of the week, you then can review your jottings to see if they reveal any patterns and if there is something you can learn from them.

NOTE
On Being Embodied

I am brought back once again to seeing how vital it is that
I take respect for myself seriously.... What if I should
discover that the person most in need of food and alms is
in fact myself? —Esther de Waal[16]

In our electronic world we sometimes forget that we are animals, that we live in bodies. These bodies put us in touch with
the world around us via our senses of touch, smell, sight, hearing, and taste. So use all of them in various ways to help you
discern the world around you.

Part of the world with which we increasingly have lost touch,
however, is ourselves, particularly our own bodies. Although
we are thoroughly embodied creatures, we often are thoroughly
unaware of ourselves. Our bodies not only affect our emotional,
spiritual, and mental lives but also provide us ways into a greater
understanding of these aspects of our lives. So we need to become
more aware of what our bodies are telling us.

Anthony de Mello's *Sadhana* offers various simple exercises
to help us in this process (see the suggested prayer resources on
page 113). However, for now try to become aware of how your
body feels: is it relaxed or tense? Do certain parts of your body
hurt? Are certain parts of your body tenser than others? Do you
feel lethargic?

If your body feels lethargic, then this tells you that the leth-
argy will make it more difficult for you to relate to God and to
other creatures. You might need to take a walk, garden, stretch,
or in some way move around to wake your body and spirit up.

---

16. Esther de Waal, *Living with Contradiction: An Introduction to Benedictine
Spirituality* (Harrisburg, PA: Morehouse, 1997), 85.

If you're tense, this agitation in a similar way impedes your receptivity. It also may tell you that something is going on in your life to which you need to give some attention, whether it be a strained relationship, anxiety over your job, fear of failure or illness, or any number of other things. You may be stressed and not even realize it—but your body knows. Follow up on these hints your body is whispering to you. They are your way out and in.

So pay attention to what your body is telling you. Notice how it feels to walk, how the air smells and feels, what little sounds surround you that you've ignored up until now, how your food feels and tastes. Let your senses open up your outer and inner worlds.

CHAPTER 3

Delight, Surprise, and Wonder

I think it pisses God off if you walk by the color purple in a field somewhere and don't notice it. People think pleasing God is all God cares about. But any fool in the world can see [he is] always trying to please us back . . . always making little surprises and springing them on us when us least expect it. —Alice Walker[17]

I was walking in the woods the other day practicing noticing, and as I gazed at the bark of an oak tree covered here and there in mosses and lichens, I saw a small, round, white lump of lichen move. Now, I had never seen that happen before—plants generally haven't moved in my presence. I touched the lichen and it was soft—and no longer moved. So I waited a while, trying to be patient, and it wiggled! Well, that did it. I gently picked it up and put it in my hand, and after awhile it started walking around. I tried to turn it over to see if it had legs, but no matter how hard I tried, I either never got it in the right position or it never chose to let me see its feet. So when it started moving around on my hand, I put my hand at eye level and peeked as best I could under the lichen, and there I spied tiny little legs. How many I couldn't tell, but legs nevertheless. The surprise and delight of that day still stay with me. I saw something wondrous and unexpected.

> "For you, O LORD, have made me glad by your work; at the works of your hands I sing for joy. (Ps. 92:4)

---

17. Alice Walker, *The Color Purple* (New York: Open Road, 2011), 353–54.

Wonder, delight, and the experience of serendipity go together, arising from the things we notice as we go through our day. When someone unexpectedly gives us a special gift, we experience delight. Delight takes us back to the days when as a child we daily discovered new things and relished the adventure. Ellen Davis points out that God's delight in creation, the work of his hands, is the hallmark of his rule over the earth.[18] And it's the hallmark of how we should relate to God's creation.

> "This [wondrous] journey is available to everyone and makes life richer and more meaningful: The lasting pleasures of contact with the natural world are not reserved for scientists, but are available to anyone who will place himself under the influence of earth, sea and sky, and their amazing life. —Rachel Carson (1907–1964)[19]

When we are surprised, we also grow a bit—the boundaries of our world stretch a little farther. We realize that the world is a bit bigger than we thought and as a result, wonder may spring up from our hearts. In the moment, we forget ourselves, swept up in an experience that captures our imagination.

> "I will extol the LORD with all my heart, . . .
> Great are the works of the LORD;
> they are pondered by all who delight in them.
> (Ps. 111:1a, 2, NIV)

---

18. Ellen F. Davis, *Scripture, Culture, and Agriculture: An Agrarian Reading of the Bible* (New York: Cambridge University Press, 2009), 64–65.
19. Rachel Carson, "The Sense of Wonder," *Women's Home Companion Magazine,* July 1956, 48.

There's a wonderful set of videos where researchers tell students to look for something particular in a scene. In one of the set of similar scenes the students are presented, a person in a gorilla suit passes by in full view. When the students are asked, "What did you see?" few of them report having seen a gorilla—they were too busy looking for something else. We see what we expect to see, hear what we expect to hear.

Thus, if we hope to experience God's wonderful works and to find God in unanticipated places, we need to be open to surprise. We need to walk with our senses wide open and our antennae out. So today when you go out, do so with no expectations as to what will happen. Ask the Holy Spirit to open your mind and heart. Be ready to be surprised. Be curious, watchful. If you see something that catches your eye or calls your attention, check it out. Spend time with it and explore. Be ready to play . . . allow yourself the joy of delight.

TAKING IT HOME

What lessons did you learn from trying to be open to surprise? How can you apply these lessons during the rest of your week? What would it take to be open to surprise? To delight in what you encounter? To open yourself to wonder? How would doing so change the way you experience life? This week try to open yourself to these things and see what happens. Record your thoughts and experiences in your journal and reflect on them at the end of the week.

> "When I have lost the gift of wonder I have ceased to live gratefully, and instead I am at war with myself, torn by greed and assertiveness, envious and discontented, ajar with everything and living an unhealed relationship with the world around me. —Esther de Waal[20]

---

20. de Waal, *Living with Contradiction*, 81.

CHAPTER 4

Appreciation and Respect

Remember the wonderful works he has done,
his miracles, and the judgments he uttered. (1 Chron. 16:12)

God clearly appreciates and delights in the works of God's hands. We sometimes may not delight in what we encounter— we can't make that happen. However, we *can* come to deeply appreciate what we meet.

By getting to know what attracts our attention and spending time with it, we can foster an appreciative attitude for it, whether it be a lichen, herb, rock, or squirrel. What does it mean for a lichen to truly be a lichen? We can admire its tenacity, living where nothing else could live. Or we can admire a stream, which flows over all obstacles or moves lithely around them. We are called to appreciate these things *for what they are* and to grow to delight in them as God does.

Appreciating things for what they are may require us to remove a few biases from our encounters with them. For instance, when I see my cat, I see "my cat Maggie," not a smaller funny-looking human being. I revel in Maggie's catness, whether or not I understand her feelings or what she is trying to tell me. Our openness and willingness to let what we encounter be what it is, apart from ourselves, helps us delight in what we find.

In another vein, I have to admit that I don't like briars—they tend to take over our woods and tear at my pants and arms. Yet many animals benefit from them. And when I remove my prejudice, I see they are beautiful plants. Yes, they can choke out other plants, but they are just doing what they are meant to do.

Choking out other plants is part of being a briar. I don't have to like that—I'm just called to appreciate that they are playing the role that they have been given. Would that I would play my role as well as they do theirs!

Appreciation involves both recognizing and relishing the differences and commonalities with those we meet. Spices transform an otherwise common dish into a memorable occasion. Difference spices up our life, even if it initially turns us off. Coming to appreciate the difference enriches us.

> "How great are your works, O Lord!
> Your thoughts are very deep! (Ps. 92:5)

At the same time, recognizing and appreciating those things we share in common can lead to empathy and a sense of kinship. Awhile ago I encountered a maple tree next to a small stream. Maples can take on amazing shapes, as did this one. It was full of lumps, which I found aesthetically pleasing. Then I realized that the maple was dealing with a viral infection that caused these deformations. At that moment, my fascination turned into empathy. It too was fighting the good fight against physical problems, just as I was. When I said goodbye to the tree, I felt I had encountered someone walking the same road as mine. The maple had become a companion with whom I shared a common experience. Appreciation leads to empathy and respect, first steps on the road to love.

Take some time to reorient and to pray before you go out. Then when you go out, notice the things about you. When you encounter something that attracts your attention, take time with it. Get to know it in all its aspects, how it relates to the things around it, accept it for what it is, and come to appreciate it. If it is a plant, for instance, consider how it gets its food, depends upon someone to pollinate its flowers, contributes food to others, and extends out of sight far beneath the ground. When you feel this particular conversation has ended, bow to it, touch it gently, or give it some other sign of respect and then move on to your next conversation partner.

TAKING IT HOME

During the week appreciate the things about you: the people you meet (even the obnoxious ones), the objects you handle, the places you inhabit. Try looking deeply into those you encounter, trying to understand and appreciate what their lives are like. Respect their difference from, and commonality with, you.

CHAPTER 5

Concentration: Getting in Touch

I remember the days of old,
> I think about all your deeds,
> I meditate on the works of your hands.
I stretch out my hands to you;
> my soul thirsts for you like a parched land. (Ps. 143:5-6)

We live in a world of sound bites, instant communication, and three sentence (or less) messages. Prolonged in-depth conversation, particularly in person, is something we increasingly experience less and less in a busy world trying to be "productive." During the day we may notice something but then pass on in a rush to get to the next thing on our agenda. Yet the most productive time we can spend often involves devoted attention or concentration to something. If we truly want to know someone or something, we have to be willing to spend time with them, time when we devote our total attention to them. By doing so, we give them a part of ourselves and, in turn, receive much in return. In this way our appreciation and respect for them grows. Giving something our total attention represents another step toward love.

Having practiced noticing and appreciation, we now must learn how to spend time with what we've encountered. Today we are going to practice a form of prayer, or if you will, an approach to life, that involves giving our total attention to something. After you have reoriented yourself, ask the Holy Spirit to guide you to something with which you will spend time. When you have found something that attracts you in some way, that calls you to it, spend twenty minutes or so with it (or more if you want) in total concentration. It will help if it's something you can get up close to and examine carefully—perhaps a rock, boulder, plant, or tree trunk. If you find your mind starting to wander, remember your intention to give all your attention to what has called you and gently return your mind and heart to it. If you are tired out from the effort, then spend the rest of your time noticing with an open heart and mind. However, if you have the energy, you may see if something else calls you to take time with it. If it does, then do so.

> " For from the greatness and the beauty of created things their original author, by analogy, is seen. (Wisdom 13:5, NABRE)

This takes practice. Should you find this difficult, don't worry. Many do, particularly in today's culture. However, cultivating the art of concentration will reward you many times over. Be patient and kind with yourself. You are learning and growing in ways that you may not even realize. Don't judge or evaluate how well you've done. Just give yourself lovingly and patiently to the practice and to the things that call you. Be open and inquisitive, ready for surprise.

As usual, after you have finished, record what happened and reflect on it.

TAKING IT HOME

In a world where we often multitask and run from thing to thing, what do we lose? How are we poorer? Many contemplatives declare that the most important thing one can do is to stand still. What would happen if you were to focus totally on whatever you were doing, were to give all your attention to the person to whom you were talking? What would it be like to patiently leave all the other things to another time when you could give them the time they too deserve? One thing to consider is whether or not all the demands on your attention equally deserve your energy. If not, then consider how you might want to prioritize among them.

> " 'You shall love the Lord your God with all your heart, and with all your soul, and with all your mind.' This is the greatest and first commandment. (Matt. 22:37–38)

Try practicing concentration at least some every day and see what happens. For instance, rather than multitask, concentrate on just one task and finish it. Then move on to the next in the same way. When you talk with someone, give them your total attention. Record the results in your journal at the end of each day.

At the end of the week, take a look at what you have written. Some questions to consider include: What challenges did you face? How might you grow in this practice? What rewards would you reap if you were to do so? What might your life look like if you were able to approach life much more consistently this way?

NOTE

On Expectations: Letting Go

"Is there anyone among you who, if your child asks for a fish, will give a snake instead of a fish? Or if the child asks for an egg, will give a scorpion? If you then, who are evil, know how to give good gifts to your children, how much more will the heavenly Father give the Holy Spirit to those who ask him!" (Luke 11:11–13)

We fill our lives with expectations. They motivate us and hinder us, depending upon what they are. If we expect good things, we work with enthusiasm and look forward to the day. If we expect the worst, we draw back and go through our day reluctantly.

We also tend to see and hear what we expect to see and hear. How many times have you had people totally misconstrue what you said because they thought you were talking about something else or because you said something unexpected? How many times did you have to repeat yourself until they finally heard what you were saying? And of course, how many times have you done the same to someone else?

All this also holds true for our relationship with God and God's creation. When we go out prayerfully, we should expect good things. As Paul says, "All things work together for good for those who love God" (Rom. 8:28). We know God wants us to get closer to Creation and to the things God so deeply loves. However, we cannot *make* anything in particular happen. In fact, if we expect something in particular to happen, we may totally miss what the Holy Spirit might be trying to do in our life right then. We need to go out with a positive attitude but with no particular expectation about what will happen. We need to "let go" of what we want to happen or "know" will happen. Whatever happens, be grateful for it, even if nothing in particular seems to have occurred or if we don't like what does. As with any form of prayer, we can never know what God will do deep within us. We can only be thankful for God's presence and action in our life. Trust that God is at work in all things.

We also may have negative expectations or attitudes about creation too. Bugs, ticks, briars, and mud do exist in nature and in other forms in our daily lives. Be aware of your fears of nature or of God that lead to negative expectations—these expectations can block you from receiving the good things God would give you today. As Matthew reminds us, God gives us good things when we ask (7:9). And, as the stories in Anthony de Mello's *The Song of the Bird* remind us, sometimes what looks like a bad thing actually may be good![21]

21. Anthony de Mello, *The Song of the Bird* (New York: Doubleday, 1984).

CHAPTER 6

Thanksgiving: The Formation of Right Attitude

O give thanks to the Lord, for he is good;
for his steadfast love endures forever. (Ps. 107:1)

After assessing her circumstances and the difficulties they brought, Helen Keller concludes, "I thank God for my handicaps, for, through them, I have found myself, my work, and my God."[22]

Daily practice of thanksgiving keeps us in touch with God: it uplifts our heart and mind, which leads to an increased awareness of God, which leads to an increased sense of creation's magnificence and appreciation for all God has created.

This deeper appreciation leads to an increased desire to give thanks to the Giver, leading to an increased awareness of God.

> "Give thanks in all circumstances; for this is the will of God in Christ Jesus for you. (1 Thess. 5:18)

Therefore, thanksgiving builds on our practices of noticing, delighting, and wondering, returning our attention to the giver of all good gifts. As such, it represents a fundamental approach to engaging the Book of Nature and to coming closer to God, as

---

22. Bill Federer, "Helen Keller 'I thank God for my handicaps, for, through them, I have found myself, my work, and my God,'" American Minute, June 27, https://myemail.constantcontact.com/JUNE-27---Helen-Keller--I-thank-God-for-my-handicaps--for--through-them--I-have-found-myself--my-work--and-my-God-.html?soid=1108762609255&aid=o8Py0MdLHMI.

well as a powerful way to reorient ourselves in the midst of our busy lives.

Activity

After you have reoriented and prayed, go out to practice thanksgiving. When you do, walk about. Be aware of your surroundings and of your body. Give thanks for the things you encounter, for all that you notice.

> "The whole world is potentially a sacrament. For it is through the material things of his world that God chooses to reveal himself. If this is so, then I should handle those things with reverence and respect, with joy, with gratitude. And when I do, I find that I am constantly aware of God the giver.
> —Esther de Waal[23]

When you return, record what happened and reflect on it. You may want to consider the following questions:

- What is easy and hard about doing this?
- What does it take to do this?
- Did I find it difficult to give thanks for some things? Why?
- Do the above scripture quotes grant us any "time-outs" from giving thanks?

TAKING IT HOME

To live gratefully re-lights my awareness and re-kindles my love, for the capacity for true sight cannot really be exercised apart from the practice of love—the capacity to see with love and delight, with wonder and tenderness, and above all with gratitude. —Esther de Waal[24]

---

23. de Waal, *Living with Contradiction*, 80.
24. Ibid., 81.

All this week practice giving thanks for all that you encounter, for all the things you do, and for all the people and objects you meet. Be grateful for the water that flows from the tap; for the make-work tasks at the office; for the people who "interrupt" your work or who bring you a kind word; for the food on your table. How does this affect the quality of your interactions and of your experience of your everyday life? How might practicing gratitude and thanksgiving change your life and the lives of those around you? Record your experiences and thoughts in your journal. At the end of the week, see what you can learn from them and reflect on the significance of these lessons.

NOTE

On Discernment
and Diamonds

At this place in our journey it might be helpful to make a couple of points.

On Discernment

First, as we have seen, all that we are doing lies upon the bedrock of being awake, of noticing. However, there is noticing and *noticing*. As people on a spiritual journey, perhaps the single most important thing we can do is to *notice* the movements of the Holy Spirit, and then respond appropriately. This requires more skill than noticing the ants going up and down a tree. In this case, we need to have our antennae out for the subtle, gentle ways the Spirit speaks to us and guides us. For instance, consider Elijah's experience in nature:

> The LORD said, "Go out and stand on the mountain in the presence of the LORD, for the LORD is about to pass by."
> Then a great and powerful wind tore the mountains apart and battered the rocks before the LORD, but the LORD was not in the wind. After the wind there was an earthquake, but the LORD was not in the earthquake. After the earthquake came a fire, but the LORD was not in the fire. After the fire came a gentle whisper. When Elijah heard it, he pulled his cloak over his face and went out and stood at the mouth of the cave. (1 Kings 19:11–13, NIV)

Elijah knew that most often God speaks with a "still, small voice," though God has been known to knock people off horses to get their attention. As you become more and more oriented toward God and quieter in your heart and mind, you may start to notice a gentle "nudge" that would incline you to go in a certain direction, to consider a new idea or course of action, to check out a certain place or plant. This subtle sense of encouragement, or of a gentle "tug at your sleeve," may be the Holy Spirit's guiding you.

The first step to discerning the movements of the Holy Spirit in your life is to notice the gentle nudges and still small whispers within you. In the context of your times of nature contemplation, the first step in learning to distinguish between these nudges and those that merely arise from your emotions and physical state is to follow them and see what happens. You may be surprised. Over time you'll learn when you hear the still, small voice of God and when you are talking to yourself. Later on we will consider how to discern the movement of the Spirit in contexts that require greater care, such as deciding what God may be speaking to you about changing jobs or healing relationships. For now, however, let's just learn to *notice*.

About Diamonds

As we go through this program, we build a series of attitudes and skills that enable us to pray unceasingly, to make our very life itself a prayer. In this way, God's life in us increasingly will shine out so that we shed his light on the world wherever we may be. Just as a master gem cutter takes a rough stone and transforms it into a multifaceted work of art that reflects light in a glittering, arresting manner, so God is creating a multifaceted work of art—you. Gratitude, wonder, appreciation, and all the other areas we work form you into that beautiful creation of God.

When you focus on one facet of a gemstone, all the other facets still appear in the background or to the side. Similarly, all the facets we have been practicing, and will practice, always work together. When you go out to practice gratitude, for instance, you can't help but practice noticing and appreciation. You may find yourself drawn to deep wonder or some other practice instead of gratitude for awhile. That's just fine. Let yourself move from facet to facet as you feel led to do so. The Holy Spirit will guide you as you move about or stay put. When in doubt, go back to the lesson for the day; for example, return to grati-tude when you feel that your deep appreciation for the rock you hold in your hand (or something else) is starting to wane. Being grateful doesn't preclude concentration or wonder or delight. They all work together and reinforce one another. In learning to be grateful, the Holy Spirit may nudge you in another direction for awhile and then bring you back to the emphasis of the day. *The Holy Spirit is your teacher.* Let it guide you on every step of your way.

JOURNEY TWO

The Road to Kinship

Lest we think that the spiritual life always involves feeling happy, we need to remember that even roses come with thorns. If we strive to make our whole life a prayer, then that necessarily involves embracing the thorns that we encounter along our path. All of creation—human and nonhuman—experiences pain and suffering. Learning how to relate to creation when it suffers, and particularly when we suffer, requires us to grow in detachment (a theme we encountered in journey one). It also develops our humility, one of the attitudes George Washington Carver identified as a key for relating to creation.

While journey two challenges us in fundamental ways, it also frees us and opens us to new dimensions of life. Paradoxically, facing difficult circumstances leads us, with God's help, to joy, something far more profound than happiness. It also deepens our sense of community, or kinship, with creation when we come to empathize with others' difficult circumstances. This journey ends by encouraging us to sit silently in amiable companionship with creation, having progressed in letting go of our own agendas and in empathizing with those around us. As such, it sets the stage for our final journey that begins with love.

CHAPTER 7

Facing Our Mortality: Letting Go a Bit More

So teach us to count our days
that we may gain a wise heart. (Ps. 90:12)

When participants in one of our introductory Opening the Book of Nature events go out for their first encounter with creation, many report that they ended up reflecting on the cycle of death and life.[25] Paradoxically, one of the major keys to unlocking the Book of Nature appears to be facing our own mortality. This paradox lies at the heart of Christianity—that death leads to life; that to live, one must die.

St. Benedict urged his monks, "Keep death daily before your eyes," as well as ". . . with the joy of holy desire . . . look forward to Holy Easter."[26] Why do we need to face our mortality if we are to learn from creation and to grow spiritually?

> " Why, do you not know, then, that the origin of all human evils, and of all baseness, and of all cowardice, is not death, but rather the fear of death? —Anonymous

There seem to be a number of reasons. We continue to learn of the importance that gratitude plays in this process. The greatest gift we have been given is life itself. Becoming aware that we have received a precious gift every morning that we get up and

---

25. *Living in an Icon* builds on our years of experience introducing people to contemplation through "Opening the Book of Nature."

26. *St. Benedict's Rule for Monasteries,* trans. Leonard J. Doyle (Collegeville, MN: The Liturgical Press, 1948), 16 & 70.

feel the morning sun leads us to thanksgiving at a most fundamental level.

When we realize that our very existence is a gift, and that in all of creation life follows death, we slowly lose our revulsion of death. Fearing death is a natural thing, but drawing back from it and holding onto life at all costs keeps us from being willing to fall into God's arms.

> "Life is given us that we may learn to die well, and we never think of it. We occupy ourselves with everything else
> —St. John Vianney[27]

Realizing that God is with us at all times, even in our dying, helps us rely more and more on God. Similarly, we like to act like little gods, believing that we've got everything under control. In reality, of course, we control very little and need to rely on God's goodness at every moment. Keeping death in front of our eyes reminds us of our utter dependence on God and keeps us focused on the Holy One. As a result, in our eyes we become smaller and God bigger, and we gain perspective on life.

When we realize that all creation passes through death to renewal, we feel more and more kinship with the world about us. We grow in empathy. We see things in a larger context. This helps us come to appreciate those things that truly fulfill and enliven us. As we cling to life less and less, we paradoxically encounter new dimensions of it. Life grows richer, freer, and more joyful. Fear occupies less space in our life the more God can replace it with joy.

> "There is no way of making a person true unless he gives up his own will. In fact, apart

---

27. Jean Vianney, *The Spirit of the Cure of Ars*, trans. M. L'Abbe Monnin (London: Burns, Lambert, and Oates, 1865), 221.

> from complete surrender of the will, there is no
> traffic with God. —Meister Eckhart[28]

When you go out today, go with the intention of facing your own mortality and that of the world about you. Remember that this might lead you to other facets of the gem we are working on, and that's to be expected.

TAKING IT HOME

As you go through your day, try to be aware of the various facets of the gift of life, such as being able to walk, see, and smell; to touch a dear friend; or to listen to music. Ask yourself: If you knew you only had today to live, what would matter most to you? What have you been learning in the rest of creation that you can apply to the rest of your day and to each day this week? How can realizing deeply your own finiteness and frailty help you live life more fully?

> " But let children walk with nature, let them see
> the beautiful blendings and communions of
> death and life, their joyous inseparable unity,
> as taught in woods and meadows, plains
> and mountains and stream of our blessed
> star, and they will learn that death is stingless
> indeed, and as beautiful as life . . . —John
> Muir[29]

---

28. Meister Eckhart, *Meister Eckhart: A Modern Translation*, trans. Raymond Bernard Blakney (New York: Harper & Brothers, 1941), 16.
29. John Muir, *A Thousand-Mile Walk to the Gulf* (Boston: Houghton Mifflin, 1916), 70–71.

CHAPTER 8

Reverence

For God so loved the world that he gave his only Son.
(John 3:16)

Near the Jordan River in ancient Palestine, the Abbot Gerasimus
healed the paw of a wild lion that became tame in his presence.

On the Irish coastal island of Iona, St. Columba wrote that he
feared the sound of an axe in the forest more than the sounds
of hell itself.

In the Italian countryside near Perugia, St. Francis of Assisi
picked up worms that strayed upon the paths after rains so they
would not be stepped upon; he set out honey for the bees in the
winter season.

Deep in the Russian forest, St. Seraphim of Sarov befriended
a bear and then other normally wild animals who thereafter
kept him company in his hermitage.

When the Celtic missionary to the European mainland St.
Columbanus journeyed into the Vosges mountains, he began
each day with morning prayers. He would call to the wild creatures and it is said that the birds would quickly fly to him.
"Then he would stroke them with his hand and caress them;
and the wild things and the birds would leap and frisk about
him for sheer happiness, jumping up on him as young dogs
jump on their masters."[30] This is what Bishop Chamnoald of
Lyons, a disciple of Columbanus, testified that he often saw
with his own eyes.

30. "St. Columbanus (543?-615)," The Orthodox Fellowship of Transfiguration,
accessed February 11, 2019, http://www.orth-transfiguration.org/resources/library/
writings-of-the-saints/st-columbanus-543-615/.

> "I do not worship matter. I worship the Creator of matter who became matter for my sake, who willed to take His abode in matter; who worked out my salvation through matter. Never will I cease honoring the matter which wrought my salvation! I honor it, but not as God. . . . Because of this I salute all remaining matter with reverence, because God has filled it with His grace and power. Through it my salvation has come to me. —St. John of Damascus (675–749)[31]

Across early and medieval Christendom, the lives of the saints are rich in accounts about respect for wild creatures and the amazing ways in which they responded to holiness and a reverent attitude. Just as notes on the musical scale repeat an octave (eight full notes) above one another, so do those approaches to creation that restore us to a right relationship with it reappear at higher (or more profound) levels. We have practiced appreciating and respecting other creatures. Our next step on the path to right relationship with God's creatures consists not only of respecting their existence, but of revering them as creatures precious in the eyes of God and revering the life of the Lord that animates every aspect of their beings. Reverence represents a higher (or deeper) octave of appreciation and respect.

> "Only by means of reverence for life can we establish a spiritual and humane relationship with both people and all living creatures within our reach.[32]

---

31. *On the Divine Images,* trans. David Anderson (New York: St. Vladimir's Seminary Press, 1980), 23.

32. Excerpt from *Albert Schweitzer Speaks Out,* reprinted from 1964 *World Book Year Book,* accessed January 8, 2019, http://home.pcisys.net/~jnf/schauth/rq7.html.

> **"**Reverence for life brings us into a spiritual relation with the world which is independent of all knowledge of the universe. It is the source of constant renewal for the individual and for mankind. —Albert Schweitzer (1875–1965)[33]

Reverence is born of humility, nurtured in love, and tempered by the knowledge that we serve our Creator who enlivens every person and every thing. All things are so precious to God that God chose to become one with creation by becoming "flesh," by becoming a created being. We sometimes forget that the word "world" in John 3:16 is really the Greek word for "cosmos," which can also be translated as "beauty" or "arrangement."[34] This passage tells us that God loves the entire created order in all its beauty so much that God gave us God's only son. Because we realize that God is everywhere and that God dearly loves all things, we hold every relationship, whether with rocks or people, with a holy regard. Reverence leads us to honor all we encounter and, at times, to respond with a sense of awe for the unseen presence of God. As St. John of Damascus says, we do not worship what we see but what we do not see; we do not worship the creatures but rather the Creator who infuses all things with its presence. We go below the surface into the mysterious depths of life and being. When we do this, the spiritual doors of nature begin to unlock.

---

33. Albert Schweitzer, *The Teaching Reverence for Life*, trans. Richard and Clara Winston (New York: Holt, Rinehart and Winston, 1965), 26.

34. John Gatta, *Making Nature Sacred: Literature, Religion, and Environment in America from the Puritans to the Present* (New York: Oxford University Press, 2004), 90. See also Robert Young's *Analytical Concordance to the Bible* (Nashville: Thomas Nelson, 1992), 1074.

Finally, reverence restores right relationship. It breaks down barriers of separation and allows for sober communication; it heals the hurts caused by arrogance and misunderstanding. Reverence cultivates awe and devotion from which sprout service, nurture, care, and love. As an attitude toward life, it opens the doors of our perception so that we come to see nature as a living book filled with inspiration and meaning.

Now imagine for a moment that someone very special to you has given you a small sculpture that they lovingly crafted with all their heart and wanted you to take along with you. They also have told you that in some mysterious way they are present in it and long to speak to you through it. This way, no matter where you are they will be able to speak to you heart-to-heart through it. How would you react to such a wonderful gift? Certainly with delight, wonder, and appreciation. I would wager that you would revere the sculpture not only as a sign of your friend's love but also because in some way your friend is there within it. It would be precious to you on various levels.

This is how we can approach creation, of which we are a part. When you go out and encounter something that attracts your attention, accept it as it is and appreciate it. Acknowledge the amazing things it does. Allow yourself to delight in what you see and to wonder. Honor its difference and its kinship with you as a fellow creature. When you have come to appreciate what you have encountered, try moving toward a stance of reverence toward it. Allow the Holy Spirit to guide you. Try looking within it to see God looking back at you from within it. When you feel your conversation has ended, find some way to honor your conversation partner (perhaps with a bow or gentle touch), and then move on to the next thing you notice.

TAKING IT HOME

In his Rule, St. Benedict enjoins his monks to treat everything at the monastery, whether tools, food, or buildings with reverence. He sums this up with one phrase: "Look upon all the tools and all the property of the monastery as if they were sacred altar vessels."[35]

As you go through your day, cultivate an attitude of respect and reverence for all you encounter, whether people, events, animals, or things. Notice when this seems easy and hard to do and jot these in your journal. Reflect on what it means to revere things that are obnoxious or even dangerous. How do you react to their presence and how might you be called to act? Why were some things easy while others were hard to revere? Finally, what might your life be like if you more consistently acted out of reverence for all you met?

> " He is the image of the invisible God, the firstborn of all creation; for in him all things in heaven and earth were created . . . all things have been created through him and for him. He himself is before all things, and in him all things hold together. (Col.1:15–17)

---

35. *Rule of St. Benedict*, 21:10.

CHAPTER 9
Hospitality

The Lord appeared to Abraham by the oaks of Mamre, as he sat at the entrance of his tent in the heat of the day. He looked up and saw three men standing near him. When he saw them, he ran from the tent entrance to meet them, and bowed down to the ground. He said, "My lord, if I find favor with you, do not pass by your servant. Let a little water be brought, and wash your feet and rest yourselves under the tree. Let me bring a little bread, that you may refresh yourselves, and after that you may pass on." (Gen. 18:1–5)

You never know when and where you might encounter God. Jesus says that when we give a cup of water to the least of his disciples, or welcome a child into our midst, we welcome him. No wonder the monks stress hospitality. I taught for several years at St. John's University, a Benedictine university. They had a way of making you feel welcome from the first time they met you. They joyfully brought us together in community celebrations, such as the Christmas festival to which all were invited and took part. They always offered food and drink, joy, and genuine warmth. It was hard to feel like an outsider for very long.

> "Do not neglect to show hospitality to strangers, for by doing that some have entertained angels without knowing it. (Heb. 13:2)

Of course, not all strangers attract us. We may not even like them. We may not like them even once we get to know them. However, we know that Christ lives in them, no matter how unattractive they may be. So we revere and respect them and offer them hospitality. Hospitality is a step toward love, benefitting us at least as much as the stranger. Hospitality pries open the door of our heart, allowing a bit of the light of God's love to enter in, as well as to venture out. After all, doors invite the outside in and the inside out.

> " Let all guests who arrive be received like Christ . . . —St. Benedict (c. 480–543)[36]

When you go out today, welcome all you meet: the glorious sky, the weeds, the water, the mosquitoes, and the briars. When you return, record your experience. Again, what did you find easy or hard to welcome? What did you learn from the experience?

TAKING IT HOME

This week practice hospitality. Welcome all you meet, whether they be people, things, events, sickness, or joy. Remember that as you notice your feelings and your interactions with others, you are encountering yourself too. We often are strangers to ourselves, or an unwelcome presence. We often dislike what we see. Yet we are called to welcome this stranger too. Practice hospitality with yourself. Accord yourself, someone within whom God resides, the same respect, reverence, and patience you give to the others you meet.

> " No one can be a good host who is not at home in his own house. Nor can I be a good host until I am rooted in my own centre. Then, and only then, have I something to give to others. —Esther de Waal[37]

36. *St. Benedict's Rule for Monasteries*, trans. Leonard J. Doyle (Collegeville, MN: The Liturgical Press, 1948), chapter 53 [p.72].

37. de Waal, *Living with Contradiction*, 85.

In your journal, record your experiences and reflect on them. How does hospitality affect your experience of your day? Be patient with yourself if you find hospitality difficult. That's part of being hospitable! How might you change, and the world about you change, as you grow in hospitality?

NOTE

Prying Open the Door
of Our Heart:
Letting Go Revisited

Have you ever tried to pick up something with your fingers closed? Or tried to receive something a friend is handing you with a clenched fist? It's pretty hard. A closed hand often reflects a closed heart. That's why people often find it helpful to pray with their hands open on their laps. That action somehow helps us open our hearts to whatever God would speak to us as we pray.

However, if we are afraid, if we live in fear of things or fear of what might happen, we go about life with closed hands, hands unable to receive what God would give us. When we are afraid, we tightly clutch onto how we think things have to be or tightly hold onto the certainty that we need to fear some likely event. But what if God has something else in mind? What if God wants to give us something good that we don't know about?

We all know someone who lives in fear that their sweetheart will decide to leave them. We may have been there ourselves. They *know* that if their sweetheart leaves, their world will fall apart. They refuse to consider seeing anyone else, even though there are other people who might be a better match. So they cling to the sweetheart in fear that they will leave, when everyone else knows they'd be far better off either alone or with someone else. Their clinging actually prolongs their unhappiness.

We may know someone who stays in an exploitive work situation because they *know* things will be worse should they quit. They refuse to explore other opportunities because they are afraid of failing or of getting into something worse. So they continue to live a miserable life, even in the presence of positive possibilities.

Another thing we clutch tightly in our hands is an unwillingness to forgive those who have wronged us. We tenaciously grasp resentment, anger, self-righteousness, and all the other things associated with our being hurt. Yet the gospel makes it clear to us that forgiving the ones who we perceive as having wronged us frees them and allows God to touch them, while at the same time freeing us. When we cling to our anger, it poisons us and closes us off from God's love and freedom, as well as hurts us physically and psychologically. Out of love for God and ourselves we need to free ourselves by forgiving those who have hurt us. It's for our own good as much as for others'.

If you find it hard to forgive, as we all do, here are some things to consider. Forgiveness involves an act of will. You may not feel loving to the one you're forgiving, but that's all right. The emotions will follow and will heal over time. If it's appropriate, let the person know you've forgiven them. However, if the person didn't know they hurt you, bringing up the hurt on your part could create a rift between you. Be prudent. Seek reconciliation and healing of your relationship. If doing this is impossible or unwise, as with someone who is deceased, then ask the Holy Spirit to be present with you as you imagine yourself in a room with Jesus and the person. Imagine forgiving them and asking their forgiveness for rejecting them. Allow God's love to flow to them and back to you. You might imagine hugging them.

In turn, we also need to acknowledge those areas in our life where we need to ask others' forgiveness. The New Testament makes it clear that before we can approach the altar of the Lord, we need first to ask forgiveness of anyone we have wronged. To communicate or commune with God, we need a clean, clear heart. Asking forgiveness from those we have hurt may require our facing aspects of ourselves that we would rather ignore. We often would rather live in a world where we couldn't possibly be in the wrong than one where we are imperfect. Facing ourselves can be truly an inconvenient truth. Yet doing so and following up by asking and giving forgiveness pries open the door of our heart.

Hospitality and forgiveness (an aspect of hospitality) offer the possibility that by changing our attitude, an unhappy situation might be redeemable. By welcoming an unwelcome situation, we change ourselves and thereby might change others. Hospitality also welcomes the possibility that we don't know everything. It challenges us to welcome the possibility that things don't have to be the way they are, to open the door to unforeseen outcomes. Hospitality helps us to welcome serendipity and uncertainty, to embrace the unknown, to walk out of the boat onto the water. Hospitality helps us open our hands to receive whatever God might offer, to let go of the things that impede the Holy Spirit's working in our lives.

Practicing hospitality, then, helps us "let go" further. It helps us detach ourselves from the things that bind us and hold us back from the things that keep us from soaring and rejoicing in God's freedom.

Notice the things that make you reluctant, the things that get in your way. They might be fears, or other emotions such as resentment, impatience, or imprudence. For instance, we might "know" that the other person totally is to blame for our unhappiness. We might fear that we will lose out if we don't act quickly. We might act without thinking because we think we know it all, or not act at all because we don't want to be bothered. Pride, impatience, or laziness can keep us from hearing God's voice. They close our hearts to what God is trying to give us.

Facing these things in ourselves can be difficult. They often lie deep within. However, Jesus didn't become one of us to make us feel comfortable—he came to transform our lives and the world we touch each day. Should we have the courage to try something new, to unlatch the locked door of our heart, God's light will enter our life. And God's creation will find a conversation partner far easier to talk to than before.

Sometimes God will bring things to your attention that may be difficult to handle on your own. This is where a prayer partner, minister, wise friend, or counselor can be very helpful. So don't be afraid to ask for help. This is another area where we can practice hospitality and humility, welcoming the fact that we are weak and that God provides us others to help us.

CHAPTER 10

Humility: Turning Outward

> Let each of you look not to your own interests, but to the
> interest of others. Let the same mind be in you that was in
> Christ Jesus,
>> who, though he was in the form of God,
>>> did not regard equality with God
>>> as something to be exploited,
>> but emptied himself,
>>> taking the form of a slave,
>>> being born in human likeness.
>> And being found in human form,
>>> he humbled himself
>>> and became obedient to the point of death—
>> even death on a cross. (Phil. 2:4-8)

I had had an interesting week. A few days earlier as I stood on
the dam of a nearby lake and watched the clouds blowing across
a brilliant open sky, I experienced my tininess in the scheme of
things. My concerns, plans, and worries dwindled to nothing as I
experienced my place in this very large cosmos, all of which God
loves. Then a couple nights later as I walked along our country
road, I encountered a salamander, deer, centipedes, katydids, an
armadillo, and snails all going about their nightly lives just as I
was. We all were going down the road together.

All too frequently when we think of humility, we think that
it involves making ourselves small and denying the gifts we
have. We think we have to put ourselves down and grovel before
God. Instead, humility, like all virtues, represents an attitude or
a positive stance before God and others. It is the *result* of our
growing God-like, not something we actively do. When we truly
act humbly, our eyes rest firmly on God and others, not on our-

selves. Should we focus on ourselves in order to "become humble," then *we* become the focus of our attention, not God. This sounds remarkably like pride, where we matter before all else.

> "To me it seems that humility is truth. I do not know whether I am humble, but I do know that I see the truth in all things. —St. Thérèse of Lisieux (1873–1897)[38]

Humility means knowing who we are and how we are situated in the world. Animals, plants, and rocks have no difficulty being humble. Ducks don't try to be fish nor do horses oaks. We, on the other hand, love to pretend to be powerful, intelligent, cool, patient, or kind when we're not. We love to think we're in control. We fool ourselves, though we don't fool God and often don't fool others.

Similarly, we recognize we live in a community of other very small creatures, acknowledging we are only one of God's many creatures that deserve respect and reverence. Humility leads us to consider our commonality—how we all struggle to survive, how we all do important things often unbeknownst to others (such as fungi decaying organic matter—if they didn't, we'd be overrun by dead tree trunks). We realize how small we are relative to all the other beings out there upon whom we depend (knowingly or not) and experience them as comm-unity ("unity with" them). Similarly, we experience empathy for, or com-passion (passion with), the creatures we encounter.

Humility ultimately consists of determinedly seeking truth at all costs, wherever it leads us. It is a profound "letting go." Humble people recognize the good and bad within themselves and their ultimate limit to their understanding when confronted

---

38. Saint Thérèse, *Saint Thérèse of Lisieux, the Little Flower of Jesus: A New and Complete Translation of L'Histoire d'une ame, with an Account of Some Favours Attributed to the Intercession of Soeur Therese*, trans. Thomas N. Taylor (London: Burns, Oates, & Washbourne, 1912), 228.

with an immense God and world. They acknowledge their infinite smallness. Thus, humble people actively acknowledge their place in the world and their finiteness before an infinite God. They accept that they control nothing and depend upon God for everything. In seeking the truth about ourselves, we acknowledge our strengths and weaknesses without clinging to them or dwelling on them. They are just facts, nothing more or less. We treat ourselves and others gently, realizing that we're all fragile and imperfect.

> " Humility at first sight seems a threatening word. . . . It seems to imply the giving up of my own will and my personhood, with its claims of full autonomy. It is asking for self-surrender. . . . But the French equivalent . . . gives a quite different sense. *Se livrer* is much more positive. It means to hand over or to deliver oneself over to, with the connotation of a freely chosen act of love. Thus to surrender is essentially a total turning to God in self-giving, a response to a gesture of love.
> —Esther de Waal[39]

Humility flows from our practice of gratitude, wonder, respect, and reverence—and of letting go. It shifts our attention from ourselves to others, motivating us to seek the truth about ourselves and about the community of creation. Humility predisposes us to listen to others in our search for truth while it strengthens our solidarity and compassion for all creation, both human and nonhuman.

Today when you go out, acknowledge your tininess before the cosmos and your kinship with all you meet. See if you can grow in your sense of community and compassion. Demonstrate in some way to whatever you encounter your respect and reverence for it, your recognition of its worth, and your common finiteness. For example, when you encounter something that has called to you, you might consider bowing to it before you spend time with it and bowing when you finish.

> "The more you forget yourself, the more Jesus will think of you. —Mother Teresa of Calcutta (1928–1997)[40]

When you return, consider some or all of the following:
- What sorts of experiences did you have?
- What challenges or difficulties did you experience?
- What enhanced or aided your ability to let go?
- How did this experience affect or change you?
- How is humility related to love? to gratitude? to wonder? to openness? to listening?

TAKING IT HOME

You might consider two activities this week. First, Jesus gives us the example of washing his disciples' feet. Look about you during the week for small ways you might be able to serve both human and nonhuman creation. If someone needs to copy something, can you do it for them? Can you share a snack with someone who is hungry? If you notice trash on the floor or the sidewalk, pick it up. Notice; be aware. Look for little ways you can wash others' feet.

---

40. Mother Teresa of Calcutta, *Life in the Spirit: Reflections, Meditations, Prayers*, ed. Kathryn Spink (San Francisco: Harper & Row, 1983), 48.

> " It is part of the discipline of humility that we
> must not spare our hand where it can perform
> a service, and that we do not assume that our
> schedule is our own to manage, but allow it
> to be arranged by God. —Dietrich Bonhoef-
> fer (1906–45)[41]

Second, in your reflection time ask yourself how you are trying to be a fish when you're really a dog (or cat or monkey). Ask
the Holy Spirit to identify areas in your life that you use to build
up your ego in ways that close you off from God and others. Ask
the Spirit which of these ways God would have you work on
now and pray that the Spirit will give you the strength to let go
of it. This can be painful and difficult, but it's the "seed falling
to the ground and dying" that Jesus talks about.[42] It may involve
letting go of what we think defines who we are. It might involve
not clinging to social, political, or even religious dogmas that we
have treated as gods. What would it mean for you to rely totally
on God for your meaning in life so that you no longer have to
expend your energy in trying to be smart, "nice," productive,
powerful, or "right"? What does it mean to be a child of God, or
to say as Paul does that "it is no longer I who live, but it is Christ
who lives in me"?[43] In other words, what would it mean to be
truly humble?

---

41. Dietrick Bonhoeffer, *Life Together,* trans. John Doberstein (New York: Harper
& Row, 1954), 99.
42. John 12:24.
43. Galatians 2:20.

CHAPTER 11

Sharing Creation's Pain

There is no faithfulness or loyalty,
>and no knowledge of God in the land.
Swearing, lying, and murder,
>and stealing and adultery break out;
>bloodshed follows bloodshed.
Therefore the land mourns,
>and all who live in it languish;
together with the wild animals
and the birds of the air,
even the fish of the sea are perishing. (Hosea 4:1b–3)

The land mourns. . . . We seldom think about its mourning. We may think about the forest we once knew or the fact we seldom see quail anymore or frogs. But chances are we don't think that the land actually mourns.

I remember going on an Opening the Book of Nature weekend at a retreat center. Much of the land around the center bore the marks of past encounters: construction waste, stunted trees, trash, briars that arise in disturbed areas. The land was mute. It was hard to hear God speak. The same thing happened when we visited a creek flowing through the part of our town that used to be the home of our African American community that for years had no sewers or running water. A Native American with us said that the land had "clammed up." Like a hurt or abused child, or a child who had witnessed a horrific scene, the land may refuse to speak to us after experiencing or encountering injustice. Just as we carry the memories and physical scars from unloving encounters with others, so does the land. We defile it by our sinfulness—by the way we treat others—whether they be human or nonhuman.

> " Do not defile yourselves in any of these ways,
> for by all these practices the nations I am
> casting out before you have defiled them-
> selves. Thus the land became defiled. (Lev.
> 18:24–25a)

Scripture makes it clear that God loves all things and walks with us in our joy and in our pain. If we are to be Godlike, we too must do as God does. This includes being with any of God's creatures who suffer and sharing their grief. Scripture also makes it clear that in order to be right with God, we need to be right with others. This means recognizing how we have hurt others and seeking to heal those wounds. Since we aren't used to thinking of a suffering nonhuman creation, let's focus on that today.

Today let's try something a bit different. For your time outside, choose, if you can, a place that has suffered from human neglect or abuse. It could be an abandoned city lot, a paved area, a strip mine, or a trashed stream. If you cannot go to some place that you feel is appropriate, then go somewhere in your imagination to a particular place that you know. Take time to reorient yourself and open yourself to God and to all around you. Ask the Holy Spirit to open you to all it would do in you and through you, and to guide you. Be attentive to its movements. Then picture in your mind what happened to and on the land, whether it was exploitive mineral extraction, stripping of its soil, or slavery. Try to experience what it experienced at those times, the feelings and even fear. Then, in quiet, allow the land to speak to you. Open yourself to feeling the pain and rejection it witnessed or experienced itself. As best you can, feel what it experienced. As an alternative or complementary practice, you may consider writing or drawing what you feel the land is speaking to you or would speak to you. Then just sit in silent solidarity with it, sharing beyond words as you would with someone deep in grief.

When you have finished, reflect in your journal about your experience.[44]

TAKING IT HOME

As you go about your day, notice the sorts of things you do, from turning on the water to brush your teeth to driving to work in your car. Reflect on the impacts your actions are having on the rest of creation, both human and nonhuman. Where does your water come from and what did it take to get it there? What was there before they built the highway or your office? Where did your food come from and how was it grown? How did electricity get to your home and where did the energy come from? Who paid what "price" when you turned on the light switch?

If this seems a bit gloomy, yes it is. The point isn't to live in gloom or to heap ashes on ourselves, but rather to prepare ourselves to reorient our attitudes and behaviors. To do that, we first must acknowledge how we are living and how it affects others, just as we must acknowledge an overly sharp tongue or hurtful actions. Only then can we be a source of healing to the world around us. Hang in there . . . there *is* hope.

---

44. A little personal note: I had an experience while writing this chapter today on my kitchen porch. Taking a break, I looked through the kitchen window and saw a butterfly, a spotted red purple or admiral, alight on my computer. In a few minutes I opened the front door to take a walk, and there was the butterfly waiting for me on the doormat. Another butterfly has flown around me since I came back to finish writing. Maybe I'm writing what I am supposed to today.

CHAPTER 12

Settling into Silence

But the LORD is in his holy temple: let all the earth keep silence before him! (Hab. 2:20)

We have been developing our ability to notice the world about us and to listen to the Holy Spirit as it whispers to us in many, often unexpected, ways. We've also discussed listening for the still small voice. To hear God speak to us through creation we need to have "ears that hear."

There are many levels of listening. The first consists of noticing the sounds about us. Another involves listening to what our bodies tell us: that we are tense or relaxed; we hurt; our stomach is upset. A more profound form of listening involves concentrating on what something is trying to tell us. More deeply yet, we quiet our hearts and minds and rest peacefully, thinking about nothing. In more profound levels we listen to the silence behind all sounds and sensations. Mystics ultimately report a silence where they totally lose a sense of themselves and experience communion with the One who is God.

Growing comfortable with silence opens us to hearing on levels we may never have experienced before, expanding the world into dimensions we didn't know existed. Silence takes us deep within ourselves and deep into the reality permeating all of creation.

> " [There is] a time to keep silence, and a time to speak. (Eccl. 3:7)

This week we will work on this dimension of our spiritual life. Find a place outdoors that calls to you and sit there. Reorient yourself to what you are trying to do. Remember your deep intention to be open to all God would speak to you. Quiet your mind by paying attention to your breath or whatever means you have chosen for this purpose. (If you are hazy on this, review the appendix on prayer on page 104). You may find that noticing itself may be a means to occupy your mind. Notice the sounds about you, the different play of light on leaves, the feel of the breeze on your skin. However, once you've noticed something, don't focus on it. Return to noticing and awareness without thinking about what you have noticed. When you feel yourself quieting, try to stop noticing and just sit. Just be. Should thoughts return, go back to your breath, word, or noticing until once more you feel yourself opening to silence.

> "O Lord, my heart is not lifted up,
>   my eyes are not raised too high;
> I do not occupy myself with things
>   too great and too marvelous for me.
> But I have calmed and quieted my soul,
>   like a weaned child with its mother;
> my soul within me is like a weaned child that
>   is with me. (Ps. 131:1–2)

As you get more proficient in silence, you occasionally may experience listening to the silence that flows through and underneath all things. You'll know it when it happens.

Don't be frustrated by thoughts and the difficulties you may experience as you grow in this practice. We all have them. Sometimes I can be very quiet and other times I can't concentrate at all. That's ok. It's part of the whole process.

Record your experience with silence and reflect on what it tells you.

TAKING IT HOME

If you haven't already, incorporate silence into your prayer time. You might want to start with ten or fifteen minutes a day as you begin this practice. Gradually increase the time as you grow more comfortable with it.

> **"**Silence is the beginning of listening, of opening ourselves to another's heart.
> —Richard Gula[45]

During the day, notice if you feel tense, harried, unfocused. If you are feeling this way, take a few minutes of quiet. Reorient, calm your thoughts and hearts, and remember your large intention to be open to God's presence all day. What would it mean to you and others if you could carry silence in your heart all day long?

---

45. Richard Gula, "The Key to Our Mission," *Give Us This Day* (Collegeville, MN: Liturgical Press, February 2017), www.giveusthisday.org. Used with permission.

Encountering
the Burning
Bush

Journey three, the last leg of our trek, builds on the foundation we have laid—learning how to wake up and to enter into a deeper relationship with creation and, in doing so, with God. The steps we have taken along this path have readied us for the most challenging and fulfilling step of all: learning how to love all things as God does. Therefore, in this journey we spend time on learning how to give and to respond fully to all those we encounter. As George Washington Carver pointed out, this most important exercise also enables us to develop what the monks call our "spiritual senses" so that we might have "eyes that see and ears that hear." While we have been preparing ourselves to love all things, we have been laying the groundwork for perceiving what lies below their surface appearance. Consequently, the journey now focuses on perceiving the beauty of God that permeates all creation and on transforming ourselves into conduits of God's presence to all we meet. The journey concludes by setting the stage for the ongoing journey of life that continues after you finish the program.

Introduction: The Love Exercises

Whoever does not love does not know God, for God is love.
(1 John 4:8)

In his biography on the life of St. Francis of Assisi (1182–1226), Thomas of Celano relates that "when the brothers were cutting wood, he would forbid them to cut down the whole tree so that it might grow up again. He also ordered the gardeners not to dig up the edges of the gardens so that wild flowers and green grasses could grow and glorify the Father of all things . . . He picked up worms so they would not be trampled on, and had honey and wine set out for the bees in the winter season. He called by the name of *brother* all animals . . ."[46]

Francis learned to see the goodness of God in every creature. The reason, says Thomas, is that he loved all created things extraordinarily. His love embraced all creatures.

> "If you ask what . . . makes a person love creatures, . . . I reply that it is compassion and a kind of natural affection. . . . A person can be fond of a dog because it obeys him faithfully. In the same way, man in his original state had a natural inclination to love animals. . . . Therefore, the greater the progress a man makes and the nearer he approaches to the state of innocence the more docile these creatures become towards him. . . . We see this in St. Francis; he overflowed with

---

46. Lawrence Cunningham, ed. Brother Francis: An Anthology of Writings by and about St. Francis of Assissi (NY: Harper & Row, 1972) 71. Adapted and translated by Cunningham from the *Vita Prima* of Thomas of Celano.

> tender compassion even for animals, because
> to some extent he had returned to the state
> of innocence. This was made clear by the
> way irrational creatures obeyed him.
> —St. Bonaventure (1217–1274)[47]

The love of Francis was no ordinary love. His was the product of a love for God pouring love back through him so that everyone and every creature who felt this love was touched, not just by Francis, but by the love of God.

So what is this love? It is not a sentimental emotion nor a syrupy outgushing of sweet words of endearment. Love is a heart-centered outpouring of openness and affection and a sacrificial giving of one's self to God and others. Love also involves a total receptivity to what one loves, a total openness and acceptance of the other as it is, a total delight in its "otherness."

To know creation, love it. The more you love it, the more it opens up to reveal the mysteries of life. St. Francis demonstrated this kind of "ecstatic love" for creatures because he was not merely loving birds or crickets or wolves, but more deeply was loving the Christ hidden in all. This deep love affirms the unity of all in Christ. Love for God then becomes a blessing to one's neighbors, human and nonhuman.

> " Love all God's creation, the whole and every
> grain of sand in it. Love every leaf, every
> ray of God's light. Love the animals, love the
> plants, love everything. If you love every-
> thing, you will perceive the divine mystery in
> things. Once you perceive it, you will begin

---

47. This exact quote is from Michael Robson, *St. Francis of Assisi: The Legend and the Life* (London: Geoffrey Chapman, 1997), 245—it is paraphrasing Bonaventure from *S. Bonaventurae Opera Omni* [The Complete Works of St. Bonaventure] (Florence: Quaracchi, 1887), 3:622.

> to comprehend it better every day. And you
> will come at last to love the whole world with
> an all-embracing love. ——Fyodor Dostoevsky
> (1821–1881)[48]

Another Francis, almost eight centuries later, also reflects on this subject. Francis Schaeffer (1912–1984), the evangelical restorer of this ancient creation-centered perspective, writes, "If I love the Lover, I love what the Lover has made. . . . If I don't love what the Lover has made . . . and really love it because He made it, do I really love the Lover at all?"[49]

George Washington Carver was one of the few modern people to apply this principle in an easily explained manner. The son of a slave, a plant scientist, and devout Christian, he said that the secret of working with flowers or plants is to love them. "When I touch a flower," he says, "I am touching infinity."[50] Carver saw flowers and all other features of the land as windows through which he could discern the face of God. For Carver, humility and expectancy had to accompany love to form a workable relationship with creation. But love came first and had to be learned. Then, creation, rightly loved, would give up its secrets.

> " Learn to love the Creator in the creature, the
> Maker in what was made. Do not let some-
> thing he has made so captivate you that you
> lose him by whom you were made yourself.
> —St. Augustine (354–430)[51]

48. Fyodor Dostoevsky, The Brothers Karamazov, trans. Constance Garnett (New York: Grosset & Dunlap, 1957), 354–55.

49. Francis Schaeffer, *Pollution and the Death of Man* (Wheaton: IL: Tyndale House Publishers, 1970), 91–92.

50. Clark, *Man Who Talks with the Flowers,* 39.

51. St. Augustine of Hippo, "Exposition of Psalm 39," [39.8], Espositions of the Psalms 33–50, The Works of St. Augustine: A Translation for the 21st Century, Part 3, Volume 16, trans. Maria Boulding, ed. John E. Rotelle (Hyde Park, NY: New City Press, 2000), 204.

The more one's love of creation deliberately links to the love that is in Jesus Christ, the more the Spirit and joy pours out. The flow at first may be no more than a trickle, a rivulet flowing from a melting snowbank. But the more one focuses on and loves the Source of love, the warmth of one's heart melts the snowbank more and more. What was a trickle grows into a gushing life-giving and revitalizing flow of water "piped in" from the Eternal Spring, which is Jesus Christ. To stay in this "Spring" requires attention. Many things may be flushed out of our subconscious in the process. If they are, ask the Holy Spirit to remind you of them later should they be important. For now, maintain your focus on allowing God's love to flow. Although this process requires only the simple willful act of staying focused on the Source of love and of letting it pour through you, this encounter can transform your life.

We will practice love in three steps, or parts, over the next three chapters.

CHAPTER 13
Giving in Love

> "Teacher, which commandment in the law is the great-
> est?" He said to him, "'You shall love the Lord your God
> with all your heart, and with all your soul, and with all
> your mind.' This is the greatest and first commandment.
> And a second is like it: 'You shall love your neighbor as
> yourself.'" (Matt. 22:36-39)

This week we will focus on what we give to creation—ourselves. Love indeed involves affection. We delight in things and respond with affection. Beyond affection love calls us to give ourselves wholeheartedly, without reservation: with our whole heart, soul, and mind. We also know that Christ calls us to love even the unlovable, to love those we see as our enemies or those that society shuns. Love therefore challenges us to open ourselves to all that we encounter, to embrace even those things we usually shy away from.

When you go out this week, give yourself to all you meet. This doesn't mean you should do unwise things, like touching poison ivy or holding bees in your hand. Neither you nor I are ready to walk on water. Loving all you meet does mean respecting and revering what you encounter, recognizing that God loves it and in some mysterious way lives within it. We love it because it might be an "angel unaware" or a burning bush. In humility open yourself to the world around you. Welcome it and give yourself wholeheartedly to everything that comes along your path.

> **"** Who, finally, is my neighbor, the companion whom I have been commanded to love as myself? . . . ["The neighbor"] is humanity and ["the neighbor"] is angel and "the neighbor" is animal and inorganic being, all that participates in being. —Reinhold Niebuhr (1892–1971)[52]

Upon your return, as you record your experience you might reflect on some or all of the following:

- What sorts of experiences did you have?
- What challenges/difficulties did you experience?
- What seemed to enhance or aid your ability to love?
- How is love related to gratitude? to forgiveness? to sacrifice?
- What impact did approaching creation with love have on you?
- What impact might approaching creation with love have on creation?

TAKING IT HOME: *ORA ET LABORA*

Mindfulness is what the monastic life teaches us. It is such a very simple thing to walk through life with my hands open, my eyes open, listening, alive in all my five senses to God breaking in again and again on my daily life. If the incarnation means anything at all it means this, that God is reaching me though the material things in the world of his creating. —Esther de Waal[53]

---

52. Quoted in H. Richard Niebuhr, *The Purpose of the Church and Its Ministry: Reflections on the Aims of Theological Education.* (New York: Harper and Row, 1956), 38.

53. de Waal, *Living with Contradiction*, 79–80.

People came from far and wide to talk with the renowned, wise Brother Lawrence. A Benedictine monk, he counseled both rich and poor. When the visitors arrived at the abbey, they often would find him at his work, washing dishes, for Brother Lawrence was the abbey's dishwasher.

Brother Lawrence epitomized the Benedictine approach to life of *ora et labora*, worship and work. Benedictines mark their day with periods of communal and private prayer interspersed with work. For the monks, both prayer and work blend together because they know that prayer enables them to encounter God in all things and that, when they encounter God as they work, they are praying. For the monastic, all of life is prayer.

A friend of mine who studied at St. Meinrad's, a Benedictine abbey and school of theology in Indiana, tells the story of arriving at the campus one day. While climbing the many steps up the long hill from the parking lot below the abbey, Phil encountered an elderly monk painting the handrail. The monk (who we'll call Brother George) lovingly and carefully caressed the rail with each stroke of the paintbrush. He took his time, giving all his attention to what he was doing. As Phil approached, Brother George looked up and greeted him warmly like a long-lost friend, even though they never had met. They talked about what brought Phil to the monastery and about his studies. When Phil finally mentioned he should be getting on to class, Brother George said he understood and bade him a heartfelt wish for a good day. Then he returned to his paintbrush, making sure each atom received a loving stroke of paint.

> " Brothers, love is a teacher; but one must know how to acquire it, for it is hard to acquire, it is dearly bought, it is won slowly by long labor. For we must love not only occasionally, for a moment, but for ever. Everyone can love

occasionally, even the wicked can. —Fyodor
Dostoevsky (1821–1881)[54]

Realizing that all things are worthy of our love and attention and that God may speak to us at any time through anything, the monks cultivate a welcoming, listening heart that embraces all things it encounters. By slowly removing the barriers to giving and receiving God's love, over time the monk becomes more and more transparent and more and more a channel of God's love.

Brother Lawrence spoke of "my God of the pots and pans," the God whom he came to know intimately by lovingly washing pots and pans as if they were Jesus's feet. Scrubbing pots and pans was his path to a life so rich that people came from all over to learn from him (and still do today; see his book included in the list of prayer resources on page 113).

This week and in the weeks to come, cultivate a heart that greets all it meets with a welcome. Every time you start a new task, remember Brother Lawrence and engage your task lovingly. Do it out of love for God. Give it all your attention—one task, one mind. Give each activity its due—multitask no longer. Wash Jesus's feet as you write and speak. Listen for God's word to you. Look for God peeking out at you from within something or in the midst of doing something. *Be* hospitality.

Don't forget to record your experiences in your journal and to reflect on them at the end of the week.

> " The Benedictine life . . . simply consists in doing the ordinary things of daily life carefully and lovingly, with the attention and the reverence that can make of them a way of prayer, a way to God. —Esther de Waal[55]

---

54. *The Brothers Karamazov*, as quoted in "Conversations and Exhortations of Father Zosima," in *The Gospel in Doestoyevsky* (Farmington, PA: Plough Books, 1988), 247–48.

55. de Waal, *Living with Contradiction*, 71.

As a variant on your *ora et labora*, consider enjoying all you do. When we encourage people, we infuse them with courage. When we enthuse someone, we "make someone interested and eagerly appreciative"[56] Similarly, we can infuse things with joy. When you do something, infuse it with joyfulness. God has given you something to do. Respond by doing it joyfully. Infusing all you do with joy is another way to bring God's presence into your consciousness and to transform your little piece of the world.

---

56. New Oxford American Dictionary, s.v, "enthuse," https://en.oxforddictio naries.com/definition/enthuse.

CHAPTER 14

Responding in Love

> Only someone who is ready for everything, who doesn't
> exclude any experience, even the most incomprehensible,
> will live the relationship with another person as some-
> thing alive and will himself sound the depths of his own
> being. —Rainer Maria Rilke[57]

You're out with your best friend, the person you're closest to in the whole world. Your friend loves you with a deep abiding love. You start sharing with them the deepest secret of your soul, something you've held back for years, never letting anyone know about it. After a few minutes, you notice that they're checking their phone for messages, not listening to what you're saying . . . and you think, *"What kind of love is this?"*

True love involves not only giving oneself totally, but also totally opening oneself to others, receiving what others are giving you and then responding with all you've got. Love leaves no compartments in one's heart—it's all one big room with open doors and windows. Love gives all its attention so that it can take in everything it meets.

Love means vulnerability. When you really open up to someone else, they may surprise you and challenge you. They might even hurt you. Love requires courage and willingness to meet the unknown. It requires open hands.

Love responds. When Kind David was bringing the Ark of the Covenant back to Jerusalem, he danced with abandon before the procession, so much so that his wife was appalled at his undignified behavior.[58] Yet God said that David was a "man after his own heart," the only person in the Bible described that

---

57. Rainer Maria Rilke, *Letters to a Young Poet,* trans. Stephen Mitchell (New York: Modern Library, 2001), 90.
58. 2 Samuel 6:14–22.

way. When love responds, it gives all it has, whether tenderness, compassion, joy, sorrow, touch, or a warm embrace.

> **"**The earth is full of the steadfast love of the LORD. (Ps. 33:5b)

Given all this, we also realize that we ourselves are worthy of the same love we give others. This creates a tension: although we need to give totally to others, doing so may drain us of all we have. So in loving ourselves, we need to keep two things in mind. First, we need to have a flowing spring within us in order to be able to offer water to those who need it. Therefore, we take care of ourselves, sometimes placing limits on how much we give at any moment so that we have something to offer in the future or to others now. Second, we may choose to limit our self-giving not out of self-preservation per se but out of love and respect for ourselves and for others. We limit ourselves out of love, not fear.

When you go out today, go out with an open, receptive heart. Love all you meet and open yourself to it. Notice your prejudices and biases and give them away. See everything with fresh eyes. Be vulnerable, allowing yourself to receive whatever God would give you. Go with an expectant heart, without expecting anything in particular to happen or that anything necessarily will happen. Should you receive something, whether a sense of delight in seeing something unexpected or a sense of sorrow at something wounded, let it into your being and respond in whatever way seems most appropriate to you. One helpful response consists of breathing in what you receive and allowing it to flow through your whole body. Then exhale your love to the creatures about you. If you encounter something wounded or in need of healing, inhale its need and engage it, and then exhale God's healing and love to it. However you respond, let it come from deep within you. Let it truly be heartfelt, engaging your whole being. Let it be loving and compassionate.

TAKING IT HOME

As you practice *ora et labora* this week, add receptivity and responsiveness to your practice. In your journal, reflect on the nature of love and what it means to love in our world today. What obstacles or challenges do you find in "practicing the presence of God" as Brother Lawrence did? How might you overcome these challenges and how might your life and the lives of those around you be richer if you do?

> "At each step of the way I discover that what matters is not what I can achieve but what I am willing to receive. At each step of the way I discover that this is the work of God, continually forming and re-forming, shaping and re-shaping. —Esther de Waal[59]

Many of us face a challenge of receiving God's love. We can believe that God loves everything but have difficulty believing in our hearts that God really does love us. Should you face this dilemma, James Martin, SJ, offers a possible solution drawn from St. Ignatius Loyola's "Spiritual Exercises." Try the following four-step meditation:

First, call to mind the blessings that God has given you, even amid your failings and sinfulness. . . . Second, pray about how God dwells in creatures and on the earth—in the plants, animals, and even rocks and minerals—and about how God dwells in you. Third, look at how God labors on the earth, helping these creatures to be sustained and grow, and also how God works in your life. Fourth, meditate on how all blessings descend from above, "as the rays come down from the sun or the rains from their source."[60]

59. de Waal, *Living with Contradiction*, 98.

60. James Martin, SJ, "Praying to Understand God's Love," *Give Us This Day* (Collegeville, MN: Liturgical Press, Feburary 2019), www.giveusthisday.org. Used with permission.

NOTE

Dancing with David: Prayer Revisited

David and all the people with him set out and went from
Baale-judah, to bring up from there the ark of God . . .
David and all the house of Israel were dancing before the
LORD with all their might, with songs and lyres and harps
and tambourines and castanets and cymbals. (2 Sam. 6:2, 5)

The Bible constantly exhorts us to praise God. That's because
God knows us well. By praising God, we focus our whole
being—body, mind, and spirit—on God and enter into communion with God. Praise engages us and brings us into God's presence. It serves as a wonderful way of centering and reorienting
so that ultimately we may enter into deep communion with God
and creation.

When we encounter God, we often may find ourselves led
into praise. All of creation praises God (consider Psalm 148 for
instance, or Jesus's assertion as he enters Jerusalem that the very
rocks will praise God if the people don't). When we enter into
communion with God, we may find ourselves entering the great
chorus of praise spontaneously arising from creation's encountering such a wonderful presence.

For now, let's examine two aspects of praise: verbal praise
and bodily praise. One effective way to enter into praise consists of telling God how much we appreciate God's greatness,
power, gentleness, kindness, goodness. It could be something as
simple as: "Praise you, God, for your great power. Praise you for
your goodness and kindness. I praise you for your faithfulness,"
and so forth. God isn't looking for speeches or eloquence. When
you start, it might feel stilted and artificial. That's okay—it's the
intention that matters. This is a way to focus and to center. Keep

at it. After awhile you may find that your emotions start to follow your mind as you focus more and more on the Lord. Stay at it long enough and you eventually may find yourself led into profound, contemplative silence. This technique can be particularly helpful when you find yourself distracted mentally or emotionally. It also gives you a language with which you can praise when you feel led into it.

King David and the crowd danced with abandon before the Ark of the Covenant as he brought it back to Jerusalem. This shows us what loving God with our whole heart, mind, and soul can look like. It's clear from scripture that it's not some bland affair. It's an exuberant, boisterous experience. Yet for many of us, we have trouble even swaying to the music at church or, God forbid, clapping along with it. We're afraid of showing emotion, particularly with our bodies, though as many point out, we seem to have no difficulty doing so when our favorite football team charges into the stadium. Yet we're called to show that same degree of enthusiasm and more when God charges into our life. If we are timid or shy in this area, this may inhibit us from fully opening ourselves to all God would do in our life. In this area we are called to humility and trust.

> "Praise the LORD!
> Sing to the LORD a new song,
>   his praise in the assembly of the faithful.
> Let Israel be glad in its Maker:
>   let the children of Zion rejoice in their King.
> (Ps. 149:1–2)

Here's a suggestion to consider. Think of the most joyful piece of music you know, whether bluegrass, rock, jazz, classical, it makes no difference. Find a place and time when you can be by yourself. Put the music on loud enough so that you can hear it easily. Breathe the music in. Let it roll around deep inside of you and move through every part of your being. Feel the rhythm and the emotions it expresses. Then start moving to it, however you like. You might sway around, hop up and down, swing your arms, or "dance like a fool." It makes no difference. Just respond with everything you've got. Express with your body what the music makes you feel. Try this whenever you have the opportunity and allow yourself the freedom that God's love brings you. In a similar vein, you may try listening to a moving spiritual song, or any song that moves you in a positive way, and singing it with all your heart. Remember that the psalms say to "make a joyful noise unto the Lord." It's the sentiment that counts, not how well we sing!

> "Rejoice in the Lord always; again I will say, Rejoice. (Phil. 4:4)

Having tried the above two things, you'll now have a vocabulary with which to praise, if you haven't had one before. When you encounter God's presence in nature, feel free when the Spirit leads you to respond by bowing, dancing, kneeling, or whatever you feel expresses what you want to express. Combine this with verbal praise if you feel led that way. The point is: respond with everything you've got. Dance with David.

CHAPTER 15

Returning God's Love

The greatest thing you can do in this life is to cultivate
and exercise compassion. . . . Life is about learning how
to flow with your basic goodness. It's about entering the
heart and making it the fount of your being. —Robert Lax
(1915–2000)[61]

This week's expansion on love is both simple and yet profound.
So far we have focused on opening ourselves to others by giv-
ing, receiving, and responding. Today we will open ourselves to
God and allow God's love to flow out from us and back into us.

As we know, God is love. That's easier often to say than to
really understand. Another way of saying this is that God is
"total relating." When we engage in a truly loving relationship,
we experience God. God becomes alive in us and flows through
us. We *enter into* God when we truly give, receive, and respond.
Relating this way truly is prayer.

Become aware of this dynamic when you go out to love what
you meet. Before you go out, take time to reorient and ask the
Holy Spirit to calm your mind and heart and to open you to
God's presence within you and around you. Then as you go out,
open yourself to God's love and allow that love to flow out to
everything you encounter. At the same time, open your heart
and mind to receive whatever other creatures (and God who also
lives within them) would give you. Respond with God's delight
and enthusiasm. As you breathe in what you encounter, breathe
out God's love. You might enter into silence, aware of opening
yourself to God's moving through you and in all about you.

---

61. John Dear, "The Wisdom of Robert Lax: Cultivate, Exercise Compassion,"
National Catholic Reporter, February 22, 2011, https://www.ncronline.org/blogs/
road-peace/wisdom-robert-lax-cultivate-exercise-compassion.

> " . . . reason as well as faith reveal to us the real presence of divine love in all creatures, and in all the events of life . . . Do we not know that by all creatures, and by every event the divine love desires to unite us to himself, that he has ordained, arranged or permitted everything about us . . . with a view to this union? . . . every moment of our lives may be a kind of communion with the divine love . . . and may produce as much fruit in our souls as that which we receive in the Communion of the Body and Blood of the Son of God . . . O great feast! O perpetual festival! —Jean Pierre de Caussade (1675–1751)[62]

If you find the above hard to sustain, take breaks where you try to love in a less demanding way, more with your own love and affection as you have in the last couple of weeks. You might practice gratitude or other practices from before. When you feel ready, then return to being a channel of God's love.

TAKING IT HOME

As you practice *ora et labora* this week, be conscious of the Holy Spirit of God flowing through, in, and about you. Ask God to identify those things that inhibit the flow of the Spirit in your life and to help you let go of them. Invite God to partner with you, to accompany you in everything you do so that you lovingly do them with God. Reflect in your journal on how this differs (or doesn't differ) from the experiences of practicing the

---

62. Jean Pierre de Caussade, *Abandonment to Divine Providence*, with Letters of Father de Caussade on the Practice of Self-Abandonment, trans. E.J. Strickland (San Francisco: Ignatius Press, 2011), 54–5.

presence of God, of praying with and through the work of the day, the last couple of weeks.

> " But when I put Christ, and Christ's love, at the centre, then that means that I say 'Yes' to recognizing that love and letting myself receive that love, standing under that great outpouring of love as I might stand in the midst of a shower of rain or a burst of sunlight. When this 'courtesy of love' becomes the most important thing in my life, then at last I am beginning to live the way of St. Benedict, which is of course simply the Christian life, that life of love which reflects the interplay between the giver and the recipient of love.
> —Esther de Waal[63]

> " Peace and love are always in us, living and working, but we are not always in peace and love . . . —Julian of Norwich (1342–c. 1416)[64]

---

63. de Waal, *Living with Contradiction*, 54.

64. This quote is from the 39th chapter of Julian's *Showings*, Classics of Western Spirituality (New York: Paulist Press, 1978), 245.

CHAPTER 16

Beauty

> An icon: an image that works in such a way that the
> beauty of the Lord pours through it, a person who lives in
> such a way that the beauty of the Lord streams through.
> —Eugene Peterson[65]

> The whole earth is a living icon of the face of God.
> —St. John of Damascus (675–749)[66]

Many of us have experienced something deep within creation
at some point in our lives, whether in a sunset, a mountain pan-
orama, or a stunning flower. Plato spoke about Beauty as *chora*,
something that calls out to you from within something. Moses
encountered Beauty from within a burning bush.

Christian writings historically connected Beauty to the nature
of God. Along with Truth and Goodness, the scriptures describe
Beauty as one of the three main characteristics, or "Transcenden-
tals," of God. Similarly, when God created the heavens and earth
and "saw that it was good," the Hebrew also could be translated,
"and God saw that it was beautiful." In other words, God recog-
nizes God's Self in Creation—God's presence shines out from
within things.

Many of us who have been shaped by the individualism,
materialism, consumerism, commercialism, and secularism of
modern life do not understand Beauty this way, even though
the idea is very old. Part of the reason is that in Western society, we associate beauty with aesthetics or some mere harmony
between mountains, trees, skies, and water, or perhaps with the

---

65. Eugene Peterson, *Leap Over a Wall: Earthy Spirituality for Everyday Christians* (San Francisco: HarperSanFrancisco, 1997), 81.
66. On the Divine Images, trans. David Anderson (New York: St. Vladimir's
Seminary Press, 1980), 23–25. Aggregate of the entire paragraph.

texture, colors, and delicacy of flowers, or of someone's features. However, for the Christian, even decaying leaves or mud can be Beautiful, for they can reveal the grace and divine energy that sustains the universe.

Thus, Beauty goes beyond the aesthetic, or the beautiful. It involves an ability to discern God's presence, to sense God's touch in all things. The more we cultivate a sense of this deeper, more inward side of Beauty, the more we find it in every leaf, every beetle, every person, and ultimately, the whole cosmos. The regular perception of Beauty takes discipline, intentionality, and practice.

> "O eternal beauty, . . . O eternal infinite Good! O mad lover! And you have need of your creature? It seems so to me, for you act as if you could not live without her, in spite of the fact that you are Life itself, and everything has life from you and nothing can have life without you. Why then are you so mad? Because you have fallen in love with what you have made! —St. Catherine of Siena (1347–1380)[67]

To perceive Beauty, we also need to leave behind many of the attitudes and behaviors that impede the flow of the Holy Spirit within us. Beauty calls us to continue to pry open the doors of our heart so that we might be receptive to whatever God might speak to us at any moment. In other words, if we are to hear God knocking at our door, we need to have "ears that hear." To grow in our ability to encounter God in creation, we must continue to notice those areas of our lives where God does not shine out from within us. As Ralph Waldo Emerson, the nineteenth-century transcendentalist, said:

---

67. Catherine and Suzanne Noffke, *The Dialogue*, Classics of Western Spirituality (New York: Paulist Press, 1980), 325.

Tho' we travel the world over to find the Beautiful,
we must have it in us, or we find it not.[68]

When you go outside this time, look for something of the natural world that catches your eye—look for a "burning bush" that arrests your attention. Be open, without an agenda. Look for something that "calls to you," something with a deep presence within it. It might be a magnificent view or a tiny pebble. It could be a rotting tree. Go deep, below surface appearances. Abide with this presence and see what happens. Spend time with it without any presuppositions as to what may or may not happen. Respond as you feel led.

Remember that you cannot make something call you. If nothing particularly calls your attention, notice the things about you that you find especially interesting or attractive for some reason. Spend time with it, without thinking about it. Just be with it. Be open.

When you return and write in your journal, if you encountered a burning bush, consider how you felt during and after your encounter. Are you in some ways different as a result?

TAKING IT HOME

As you go about this week, look for Beauty around you. Take time as you walk, talk, and work. Practice *ora et labora*, this time looking for God peeking out at you at unexpected times. You never know when the "angel unawares" may call out to you, so make your day a practice of expectant seeking.

If you find it difficult to do this, reflect on what attitudes or behaviors are getting in your way and ask the Holy Spirit to change you and to help you cooperate in that process. As Trappist monk Thomas Merton said:

---

68. This quote is from the essay "Art" in Emerson's *Essays and Lectures,* Library of America ed. (New York: Penguin, 1983), 435.

One of the most important—and most neglected—elements in the beginnings of the interior life is the ability to respond to reality, to see the value and beauty in ordinary things, to come alive to the splendor that is all around us.[69]

69. Thomas Merton, "Reality, Art, & Prayer," *Commonweal*, March 25, 1955, https://www.commonwealmagazine.org/reality-art-prayer.

NOTE

Healing Prayer

Bless the LORD, O my soul,
>and all that is within me,
bless his holy name.
Bless the LORD, O my soul,
>and do not forget all his benefits—
who forgives all your iniquity,
>who heals all your diseases,
who redeems your life from the Pit,
>who crowns you with steadfast love and mercy,
who satisfies you with good as long as you live
>so that your youth is renewed like the eagle's.
(Ps. 103:1–5)

Because our mind, emotions, spirit, and body all affect one another, we need a healthy mind and body in order to fully grow in our spiritual life. We need to do those things that contribute to their health, whether it be a good diet, exercise, sufficient sleep, or time with friends.

This week, let us focus on the role of prayer and health. Science is increasingly showing that a good prayer life contributes to mental and physical health. However, we can also pray for healing of our thoughts and emotions, and of our bodies. That is what we will explore briefly here.

All of us have been wounded emotionally at some time in our past by painful life events, such as the death of a loved one or receiving barbed criticism. We carry these scars with us, often for decades. They keep us from being spiritually agile and lithe, preventing us from reaching out and risking being hurt again. No wonder that Jesus said over and over again, "Do not be afraid."

While psychologists and counselors can play a critical role in healing us of trauma, just as doctors do for the body, so can prayer. There is a huge body of Christian literature on this subject for you to explore. Here are a few suggestions as to how you might pray for healing of painful memories.

Reorient yourself. Become quiet and come into the Lord's presence. Ask the Holy Spirit to guide you. Picture the incident in your mind, such as the time someone you trusted and depended upon said something hurtful to you. See yourself and the person. Only this time picture Jesus at your side. As you hear the words that brought you pain, Jesus steps between you and the other person and receives the words instead of you. Allow that reality to sink into you and allow Jesus to take the pain you once bore. Picture Jesus reconciling you and your friend, bringing peace and understanding between you. If it is helpful, you might imagine talking with your friend while in this scene, allowing the Holy Spirit to bring healing to you and your relationship.

You also can ask the Holy Spirit to shine its healing light into those portions of your spirit that are wounded. In quiet, allow the Holy Spirit to move into the depths of your soul and touch those parts that are wounded and to heal them with its loving touch. Be open to all the Spirit would do. It might ask you to forgive the other, bring to mind other memories in need of healing, or just to sit in total openness to its work.

Some deep-seated memories may require repeated sessions for healing to occur. Just as bodies typically don't heal overnight, neither does our spirit. It can take time. But God does answer prayer and God truly desires that we be whole.

In a similar manner, you can pray for the healing of someone's body by envisioning the Holy Spirit going into a broken bone, for instance, and knitting it back together. Be as open and transparent to God as possible, allowing yourself to serve as a conduit of God's healing presence that then flows into the bone. Remember that healing isn't up to you. God does it as God wills. Let go of results and allow God's love, however it will manifest itself, to flow through you.

There are many ways that Christians traditionally have prayed for healing. What matters most is that one simply trust in God and leave the results to God. God indeed does wonders, in God's time and in God's ways. Just as you cannot make Beauty appear, we cannot make God heal. However, we can know and trust that God loves all things and will lovingly touch and heal us and our world.

CHAPTER 17
Radiating Beauty

Look to [the Lord], and be radiant. (Ps. 34:5)

Fyodor Dostoevsky, a nineteenth-century novelist writing in response to the deepening ills of his day, claimed famously that "Beauty will save the world."[70] What did he mean by that? Why did he say that? This week we will practice radiating Beauty to the world about us and perhaps learn a bit about what Dostoevsky was asserting.

Today reorient yourself and use whatever practices best open your heart and mind and make you receptive to all you encounter. Pray that the Holy Spirit will guide and assist you in this exercise. Then, try one or both of the following:

1. As you move about, be attentive to God's calling out to you from within something as you did last time. When that happens, breathe the Beauty in and let it flow throughout your body. Then let it flow back out of you into the world. Become a conduit of Beauty—receiving it, absorbing it in every part of your being, and radiating it out to the world. In this way you become more fully part of the great Beauty cycle.

2. As you move about, if you are not perceiving Beauty calling to you, allow the Beauty that resides within you to radiate out to the world. You are as much part of creation as everything else you see. You too are Beautiful. Open yourself to the Beauty within you and allow it to freely flow out of you to all you meet. If you encounter resistance to the flow, note your feelings and any thoughts that may be impeding that

---

70. Fyodor Dostoevsky, *The Idiot*, trans. Constance Garnett (New York: Bantam, 1981), 370.

flow and use the practices you have been working on in the lessons and notes to allow the Spirit to move freely within and through you and then out to the world.

> " Beauty in bird and flower, in rock and cloud; in ocean and mountain, in star and sand; in storm and meadow, in laughter and play. But most exquisitely beauty in the human body with its fulfillment in the human face. Beauty releases light into our awareness so that we're conscious of the beauty of the Lord. 'It makes an icon of us all. Each of us becomes a work of art, reflecting God's glory.'
> —Anthony Ugolnik[71]

When you return, note in your journal your experiences today. How did it feel? What happened? Did you find it difficult? If so, ask the Holy Spirit to help you identify why and to help you to grow accordingly.

TAKING IT HOME

During the week try applying the above two practices throughout the day. Reflect periodically on what it is like when you find yourself more successfully applying them. How does radiating Beauty relate to radiating peace and love? How does living out of a place of deep quiet or silence correspond to radiating Beauty? Why does it require us to take out time during the day and give all things their due portion of our attention? How does it relate to *ora et labora*?

If you were to live this way more often in your life, how would it affect what you do and how you do it? What difference would it make? Why do you think Dostoevsky made his claim?

---

71. Anthony Ugolnik, *The Illuminating Icon* (Grand Rapids, MI: William B. Eerdmans, 1989), 188. Quoted by Peterson, *Leap Over a Wall*, 86.

> "It seems so much easier in these days to live morally than to live beautifully. Lots of us manage to exist for years without ever sinning against society, but we sin against loveliness every hour of the day. —Evelyn Underhill[72]

Many contemplatives say that the most important thing we can do is to stand still. What are they driving at? Is this an excuse for doing nothing or rather a radical rethinking of how we go about making a difference in the world? If the latter, how so? Author Kaleeg Hainsworth said:

I find it truly consoling that beauty is a gift to the poorest along with the richest, and that every beautiful thing is of equal value and of no value at once. I don't need to be holy to see it, but I am made holy when I do, and I am humbled in its presence because I see that God is beautiful and made me and you beautiful too.[73]

72. Quoted in Margaret Cropper, *The Life of Evelyn Underhill* (Woodstock, VT: Skylight Paths, 2003), 23.

73. Kaleeg Hainsworth, *An Altar in the Wilderness: An RMB Manifesto* (Victoria, BC: Rocky Mountain Books, 2014), 47.

CHAPTER 18

Revealing the Children of God

> Then Jesus went about all the cities and villages . . .
> proclaiming the good news of the kingdom, and
> curing every disease and every sickness. When he
> saw the crowds, he had compassion for them, because
> they were harassed and helpless, like sheep without
> a shepherd. (Matt. 9:35–36)

Have you ever sat in the presence of someone who made you feel better just by being around them? Who radiated a sense of wholeness, peace, and goodness? Who somehow made the world right, at least for the moment?

We've explored aspects of this already by working on radiating Beauty and love, on healing and forgiveness. What would it mean to reveal God to all of creation, so that when we entered a garden, woods, or beach the trees and waves would "clap their hands for joy"?

> " For the creation waits with eager longing
> for the revealing of the children of God.
> (Rom. 8:19)

Whether or not we think the Bible is speaking poetically here (there are no small number of scholars who think that the biblical writers truly were pointing to a deep reality), our human experience of how others affect us should give us the motivation to believe that indeed we can make a difference to all of creation. As the quote from Romans suggests, Paul certainly thought so. We believe in a God who is relationship itself, who is Love. To the extent we heal our relationship with all of creation, to that extent God flows more freely through it. Our faith calls us to believe that this indeed matters and to act accordingly.

God calls us to be good shepherds of creation, to be the image of God's love to all God has made, to reveal Jesus to a suffering world. What does this imply for us? Let's explore briefly how we might more fully reveal God to all of creation and bring healing to a broken world, focusing this time on the nonhuman world.

First, because we are in a relationship with creation, we must assure ourselves that our relationship with it is whole, or "holy." This means we both need to ask forgiveness of it and to grant forgiveness to it. We can ask creation to forgive us for the ills that we directly or indirectly inflict on it, such as the toxins leaking from our landfills, the exhaust we put into the air as we drive, the coal we extract and burn as we turn on our lights. To right the wrongs we engage in, we need to voice our sorrow and ask forgiveness from creation and from God. We also need to forgive creation when it harms us. When a virus threatens our life, we need to forgive it even as we fight the illness. When a flood destroys our home or crops, we need to realize that the river is just being a river and forgive it accordingly. We also might consider to what extent humans have made the flooding worse by the way we have affected the river's watershed. We may be partially to blame for the river's behavior. This will help us have compassion for the very entity that has hurt us.

We also can pray for healing. Agnes Sanford, known internationally for her powerful healing ministry for mind and body, later in life started leading people to pray for the earth. Toward the end of her life, she bought a home on the San Andreas fault and led people over the fault, praying at any spot where they discerned trouble. If a woman of great faith and conviction could approach such a large problem with a faithful heart, so can we. Although we certainly need to change our behaviors to lessen our impact on our nonhuman neighbors, that doesn't preclude our asking the Lord's help to heal the earth of the effects of our actions. Again, how we pray matters much less than that we do so. As good shepherds of creation, we too can have compassion on the helpless and harassed and heal their illnesses.

Finally, we can heal just by our presence, by radiating Beauty and Love to everything around us. We can reveal the children of God, bringing hope and joy into a suffering world.

> 66 The soul, which is created quick to love, responds to everything that pleases, just as soon as beauty wakens it to act. —Dante Alighieri (1265–1321)[74]

Today, therefore, let's work on letting God radiate from us in compassion and hope. Take some time to reorient, allowing God's presence to fill you. Become aware of God around you and in you. Ask the Holy Spirit to help you be a channel of God's healing love to all you meet. You may want to do this where you went earlier to experience the pain of creation. Or you may decide to start with a less challenging site and work your way up to that one. Let the Holy Spirit guide you on this.

As you go out, ask forgiveness of the land, water, and air for the things you have done directly or indirectly to hurt it. In God's presence accept their forgiveness and allow it to sink deeply within you. As you do with prayer for inner healing, in your imagination you might see yourself receiving forgiveness from Jesus and from the land. Allow both your mind and heart to receive it. Remember that the earth will forgive you if you truly ask forgiveness because the earth places no barriers to God acting within and through it. We're the ones who get in the way of God's moving, not the rest of creation.

Once you've righted your relationship, then walk as Jesus walked. Realize Jesus is walking along with you. After all, Jesus is Emmanuel, God *with* us. Allow God's presence to radiate out

---

74. Dante Alighieri, "Purgatorio," in *The Divine Comedy*, trans. Allen Mandelbaum, Everyman Library ed. (New York; A.A. Knopf, 1992), 298, canto 18, lines 19–21.

from you to all things. This isn't something you *do* as much as something you *are*. If you feel called to pray for the place or something specific requiring healing, do so, allowing the Holy Spirit to flow. Again, don't worry about what you do or what happens or doesn't happen.

TAKING IT HOME

Once again, practice opening yourself to God's presence in the world around you and letting God radiate from you out to all you meet. Take your time. Enjoy all you meet and appreciate all you notice. Let love and God's joy flow from deep within you. Serve what you meet. Pray for healing if you feel drawn to do so. In your prayer time ask the Holy Spirit to lead you in asking forgiveness of specific parts of creation and interceding for them. In other words, practice revealing your being a child of God to the world.

CHAPTER 19

Faith, Vision, and Hope

> Trust in the LORD with all your heart,
> on your own intelligence do not rely;
> In all your ways be mindful of him,
> and he will make straight your paths.
> (Prov. 3:5-6, NABRE)

Here we are on our last foray into the woods together. Where do we go from here?

We've spent weeks putting building blocks of a spiritual life together. We've worked on discernment of the Holy Spirit's small voice leading us, on truly listening and seeing, on letting go of those things that hold us back from experiencing the presence of God and from being all that we can be. We have explored what it means to be loved and to love, as well as to *be* love. In all this we implicitly have been growing in faith and hope.

After Jesus talked to a crowd about doing the work of God, someone came up to him and asked, "And what is the work of God?" In other words, how do we know what work God wants us to do? Jesus replied, "Believe in him whom he sent" (John 6:29). Now Jesus wasn't asking them to believe intellectually that he exists. They knew that already. He called them to trust radically in his goodness and care for them, to have confidence in his leadership.

Trust flows out of our experience of a loving God. Trusting in God is like sitting on Mommy's or Daddy's lap when we are children. As we gaze on the world from their laps, all is right in the world, even after a scary event. Mommy's lap is *home*. It's a safe place. She can make everything right. So can Daddy. And he's bigger than any bully out there. When we are cradled in love, we implicitly trust in the goodness and strength of our parent. So it is with God.

> " For the LORD's word is upright;
> all his works are trustworthy.
> (Ps. 33:4, NABRE)

If we can learn over time to sit on God's lap, we experience hope for ourselves, our family and friends, and for a suffering creation. Although we may not see the solution or the way out, Daddy's the most powerful, knowledgeable person around. We can trust that, somehow, our God knows how to make all things right. So we live in hope even despite sometimes overwhelming evidence that everything seems to be going wrong. We live, not as naïvely optimistic Pollyannas, but as people who believe that God will wipe away every tear from every eye.

We have been practicing trust all along on our journeys together. When we go out to the woods to seek God, we exercise our trust that God indeed will speak to us in often surprising ways. We go with an open heart and mind. Similarly, as we go out into our everyday world, we do so with the expectation that God will speak to us there too and lead us if we but look for the Spirit's guidance. Our attitude of expectant wakefulness presupposes trust and hope.

> " Genuine faith is courageous trust in God's
> trustworthiness. —Br. David Steindl-Rast[75]

Similarly, when we thank God for everything we encounter, whether pleasant or otherwise, we exercise trust in God's goodness. When we thank and praise God for ticks and mosquitoes, or for illness and disappointment, we exercise courageous trust in a God who says that by trusting God all things can result in good and that Jesus will walk with us in our difficulty.

Finally, when we radiate God's love and beauty to the world, we allow others the opportunity to encounter a loving God, an

---

75. David Steindl-Rast, *A Listening Heart* (New York: Crossroad, 1999), 40.

encounter that invites them to participate in a relationship of trusting love.

As we go out today, exercise faith that God will continue to guide you and will lead you to use the tools, or practices, that will most help you. Let the Spirit guide you from moment to moment as to what to notice and whether to move or stay, as to how best to open yourself to God's presence, whether it be via gratitude, giving love, reflection, or silent communion. Go out in expectant hope, sitting on God's lap.

TAKING IT HOME

Where there is no vision, the people perish.
(Prov. 29:18, KJV)

You now have a complete diamond with all its major facets in place. You will spend the rest of your life perfecting it and polishing its many facets. Continue to seek the Holy Spirit's guidance. Be mindful of God in all you do. Keep your spirit peaceful, "like a weaned child with its mother" (Ps. 131:2). Exercise trust. This is God's will for all of us.

When we care a lot about something—a project, cause, concern—we may feel that it is up to us to make it happen. We may pray that God would bless our efforts while sincerely believing that the results hang on what we do. Psalm 127 reminds us, though, that "unless the LORD builds the house, those who build it labor in vain." The Lord is the contractor. We just follow directions.

This realization leads to a core aspect of faith—playfulness. Jesus famously said, "Truly I tell you, unless you change and become like children, you will never enter the kingdom of heaven" (Matt. 18:3). In a healthy family, children know mommy and daddy are so big that they can take care of anything. They trust implicitly and as a result engage their world with gusto and curiosity. They let go and play. This is what Jesus wants of us—to let go of the illusion that it all is up to us and to trust him so much that we can engage life like a little child. So if you find yourself on a crusade, try taking half an hour a day or week and do something fun, something that works toward no goal, something that helps you forget yourself and let go of your self-importance. This can be very helpful in developing one's faith.

God also calls us to be a people of hope, to be a people who bring hope to a world wrought with war, hunger, displacement, and widespread environmental destruction that often lies behind the social turmoil we so worry about. What hope can we offer the world?

First, we have the promise that the kingdom of God is breaking forth in our midst. Hopefully we have experienced that to some degree in the last weeks as we have grown in discerning God's presence and the Spirit's work in surprising ways and places. God transforms hearts and minds. God heals all things. We can cooperate in bringing that about if we stand still long enough to become instruments of that healing. We can practice looking for God's goodness and activity when the world about us looks dark.

> "O Lord, my heart is not lifted up,
>   my eyes are not raised too high;
> I do not occupy myself with things
> too great and too marvelous for me.
> But I have calmed and quieted my soul,
>   like a weaned child with its mother;
>   my soul is like the weaned child that is
>   with me. (Ps. 131:1–2)

Second, we can bring a vision of what the kingdom may look like, what a renewed Earth could be. I remember a talk I heard at an international conference of economists and ecologists from all over the world, all people concerned about the impact that a worsening environment has on people. Donella Meadows, a prominent environmental scientist, gave one of the talks. She asked this large, distinguished, highly technically proficient crowd of people to close their eyes for five minutes and to imagine every detail of what a sustainable world might look like. She asked us to imagine waking up and seeing what our bedroom looks like, what we eat for breakfast, how we get to work, what work we do, what the workplace looks like, how we relate to people and what these relationships look like, and so on throughout the day. For five minutes thousands of highly educated people sat in total silence. At the end she urged us to do this every day, saying that unless we did so, we would have no idea as to what direction to move in nor would we have the motivation to change. Of all the talks given at this international congress, the evaluations revealed that the participants rated her talk as the most significant. Vision gives us hope.

So spend time envisioning what the world *could* look like if we truly allowed God's beauty to permeate everything we do, say, make, or grow. How would radiating God's beauty through the work of our hands change the world? How would the world be more just and loving? You will find this elevates your awareness and will motivate you to image God's love to the world through the way you live it every day.[76]

Finally, keep up the practice of going out into God's creation as often as you can. Even if you are busy and don't feel you can spend the time, if you do go out you in all likelihood will be grateful that you did so. My wife and I have found it very fruitful

---

76. Green, or ecological, design offers us a way to embody many of our values in the way we go about interacting with the rest of creation. Its values and goals in many ways echo those that permeate the gospel. An internet search on green building, ecological design, or other such topics quickly will bring you many helpful resources. You also can read Robert's article "Beauty by Design" in the December 2014 issue of the *Sewanee Theological Review* for a discussion of why the way we interact with the world matters, and how green design in many ways mirrors the values implicit in seeing God's Beauty in all things. Note that this touches both issues of social justice and the environment. For more information on why sustainable societies matter from a biblical perspective and what this might entail, you might look at Robert's book, *Economics, Ecology and the Roots of Western Faith: Perspectives from the Garden* (Lanham, MD: Rowman & Littlefield, 1995).

to spend forty-five minutes to an hour each week where we individually go out into our woods at the same time and then share with one another what we experienced. You also may want to consider some of the optional activities in the next chapter.

> All Christian life is meant to be at the same time profoundly contemplative and rich in active work. . . . It is true that we are called to create a better world. But we are first of all called to a more immediate and exalted task: that of creating our own lives. In doing this, we act as co-workers with God. We take our place in the great work of mankind, since in effect the creation of our own destiny, in God, is impossible in pure isolation. Each one of us works out his own destiny in inseparable union with all those others with whom God has willed us to live. We share with one another the creative work of living in the world. And it is through our struggle with material reality, with nature, that we help one another create at the same time our own destiny and a new world for our descendants.[77]

---

77. Thomas Merton, *Love and Living,* ed. Naomi Burton Stone and Patrick Hart, OSCO (New York: Farrar, Straus, Girous, 1979), 159.

CHAPTER 20
Who Is My Neighbor?

This chapter offers you three optional activities you can use after you have finished the other chapters. Of course, you can use them along with the earlier chapters should you choose to do so.

Getting to Know You

Have you felt God speak to you differently while looking out over a mountain valley versus sitting next to a creek nestled in the woods? Or do you feel different standing on the beach and looking out over the ocean than when walking through a beautiful garden?

Different landscapes possess different charisms or gifts—they speak to us in different ways. In similar ways any piece of land, whether a backyard or a 200-acre tract has parts that will also touch us in varying ways. Getting to know a piece of land and its character involves coming to know the ways its different parts speak to you. The more you know the land, the deeper your relationship will be and the closer your tie with it.

Reorient yourself and ask the Spirit to guide you. Then go out either alone or with someone else and walk the land. Note how you respond to different parts of it. Generally these areas will correspond to different topographic elements (such as creek bottoms and hills) of the area or different ways certain places have been managed. Draw a map of the land that outlines the boundaries of those areas that seem different to you.

For instance, our 20-acre homesite is a long rectangle with one short side fronting on a road. The area fronting the road includes a part that has the understory cleared away, our house and its immediate surroundings, and a pond. Each of these feels different to my wife and me, so we outlined these as distinct areas on a hand-drawn map.

Below our house is a field that houses a garden. Woods enclose the field on three sides. Below that a couple of creeks wind through the woods. We identified the field and creek bottoms and their neighboring ridges as places that affect us differently and marked them on the map. Soon we had a map of our land divided into sections, each of which seemed distinct to us.

Once a week we went out alone at the same time to different areas on our land and spent time there, allowing God to speak to us through places on our land. Afterward we compared notes and kept a record of our experiences. Two things happened. We came to know and appreciate the spiritual nuances of our land far more than before. We also noticed a lot more about the land itself—certain trees, plants, and habitats we never noticed before.

You might try the same, going out at different times of day in different kinds of weather. Going out at night offers a totally different kind of experience, as does being on the land in the rain. You can do this in a small backyard or a park. Even small places have different nooks and intimate places. Look for them and get to know them.

A variant of this process involves getting to know the overall charisms of different types of landscapes. Spend time if you are able to open yourself to the Book of Nature at a quiet beach, the open plains, or a mountain range. What do you tend to experience in each place? If you travel, you may notice, for example, that one landscape may tend to speak to you of God's nurturing care, another of God's awesome power, another of God's timelessness.

And Who Is My Neighbor?

Have you noticed how knowing someone's name can make a lot of difference in a relationship? Just knowing the names of the people about us and a little bit about them enriches our life and deepens a sense of belonging to a community or a particular place.

The same holds true for the community of life of which we are a part. Try this: Get to know how to identify, say, the five most common tree species where you live, along with the five most prevalent mammals and bird species. Learn the calls of the most common birds so you will be able to know that a cardinal or robin is nearby even when you can't see it. Knowing the most common wildflowers that bloom in the spring and fall can bring you great joy as you recognize them by name.

Many state wildlife resources agencies offer brochures and online resources that can help you know what to look for. There are excellent field guides such as the Peterson, Audubon, and Sibley series that provide a wealth of information. Many websites, such as the Cornell Ornithology Laboratory[78] site, provide easy-to-use resources to guide you. Or just inquire who around your area knows a lot about nature and ask them for help. They'll be glad to respond.

Digging into Scripture

Many of us, even those of us who have read the Bible for years, possess a spotty knowledge of scripture. It's a big book! The better we know the scriptures, the richer our spiritual life becomes.

Try reading through the entire Bible in one year. You will find numerous online and printed Bible reading plans to do exactly that. You might look for passages with an environmental aspect. Remember that the phrase "God's works" refers not only to God's actions in history but all the things God has made. Many passages refer to land. Every day summarize in your own words what you have read. At the end of the year, not only will have you read parts of the Bible you may never have read or that you have forgotten, but you also will have put into your own words the entire Bible as well as increased your knowledge as to how God relates to God's creation. By summarizing your reading, you may find that you remember far more of what you have read and made more sense of it too.

---

78. http://www.birds.cornell.edu.

Initial Reflections

The scriptures declare that creation is a potent witness to the Creator. The saints from every century teach that nature is a source of learning, equal to the scriptures. Yet it is no longer taught. The following quotes and excerpts remind us of this potential. The challenge for you is to recover a practical understanding of the process.

"Some people, in order to discover God, read books. But there is a great book: the very appearance of created things. Look above you! Look below you! Note it. Read it. God, whom you want to discover, never wrote that book with ink. Instead He set before your eyes the things that He had made. Can you ask for a louder voice than that? Why, heaven and earth shout to you: 'God made me!'" —St. Augustine (354–430)[79]

"The whole earth is a living icon of the face of God." —St. John of Damascus (675–749)[80]

"But ask the animals, and they will teach you; the birds of the air, and they will tell you; ask the plants of the earth, and they will teach you; and the fish of the sea will declare to you. Who among all these does not know that the hand of the LORD has done this?" (Job 12:7–9)

---

79. Vernon J. Bourke, trans. and ed., *The Essential Augustine* (Indianapolis: Hackett, 1974), 123. The text is from Sermon 126.6 in the Angelo Mai collection of Augustine's sermons, *Miscellanea Agustiniana*, ed. G. Morin (Rome, 1930), 1:355–68.

80. *On the Divine Images*, 23–25. Aggregate of the entire paragraph.

"Believe one who have experience: you will find something much more labouring [greater] amongst the woods than you ever will amongst books. Woods and stones will teach you what you can never hear from any master." —St. Bernard of Claivaux (1098–1179)[81]

"It was the Book of Nature, written by the finger of God, which I studied. . . . Nature is the universal teacher. Whatever we cannot learn from the external appearance of nature, we can learn from her spirit. Both are one. Everything is taught by Nature to her disciple if he asks for information in the appropriate manner." —Paracelsus, father of modern pharmacology (1493–1541)[82]

"God writes the Gospel, not in the Bible alone, but also on the trees, and in the flowers, and clouds, and stars." —Martin Luther (1483–1546)[83]

"I wish you could come here [to Yosemite] and rest a year in the simple unmingled Love fountains of God. You would return to your scholars with fresh truth gathered and absorbed from pines and waterfalls and deep singing winds, and you would find that they all sang of fountain Love just as did Jesus Christ and all of pure God manifest in whatever form." —John Muir (1838–1914)[84]

81. "Letter 107: To Henry Murdac," *The Letters of St. Bernard*, trans. Bruno Scott James (London: Burns & Oates, 1953), 156.

82. Before the ellipsis is from p. 20, and the final part is from p. 106 of Francis Hartmann's *The Life of Phillipus Theophrastus Bombast[us] of Hohenheim Known by the Name of Paracelsus and the Substance of His Teachings Concerning Cosmology, Anthropology, Pneumatology, Magic and Sorcery, Medicine, Alchemy and Astrology, Philosophy and Theosophy Extracted and Translated from His Rare and Extensive Works and from Some Unpublished Manuscripts* (London: Kegan Paul, Trench, Treubner & Co. Ltd., 1896).

83. Quoted from Caesar Johnson, ed., *To See a World in a Grain of Sand* (Norwalk, CT: C. R. Gibson, 1972), 24.

84. Letter from John Muir to Catharine Merrill, June 9, 1872, http://content.cdlib.org/ark:/13030/kt800035hc/?layout=metadata&brand=calisphere.

"How do I talk to a little flower? Through it I talk to the Infinite. And what is the Infinite? It is that silent, small force. It isn't the outer physical contact. No, it isn't that. The infinite is not confined in the visible world. . . . It is that still small voice that calls up the fairies" —George Washington Carver (1864–1943)[85]

"Throughout the entire creation, the wisdom of God shines forth . . . as in a mirror containing the beauty of all forms and lights and as in a book in which all things are written according to the deep secrets of God." —St. Bonaventure (1217–1274)[86]

"It is the wisdom of men to search out God's works, and to set their minds wholly upon them. And God has also ordained the world to be like a theater upon which to behold his goodness, righteousness, power and wisdom." —John Calvin (1509–1564)[87]

---

85. Clark, *The Man Who Talks with the Flowers*, 44.
86. *Tree of Life (L'Arbre de Vie)* 12:46.
87. Sermon on Ephesians 3:9–12, CO 51:462, as quoted in Susan Schreiner, *The Theater of His Glory: Nature and Natural Order in the Thought of John Calvin* (Grand Rapids, MI: Baker Books, 1995), 113.

APPENDIX TWO

Thinking about Prayer and Water

We have said that we will be working on making our whole lives a prayer that we might "pray without ceasing." So what is prayer? And how can we do it all day when we have a myriad of demands on our lives and attention?

Well, prayer simply consists of communicating with God. We can pray, therefore, actively or unconsciously. Just as we can speak to friends or unwittingly reveal our inmost thoughts via the tone of our voice or body language, so can we communicate with God through our attitudes, thoughts, and actions. It's a matter of *how* we live our daily lives.

God always wants to be in touch with us. I like to say that God is a "Mad Lover" who always desires our intimacy. Therefore, God always speaks with us. It's a matter of whether or not we're online or offline, whether or not we're ready to listen.

Prayer involves intentionality, both active and foundational. Let's take a moment to look at this distinction. We can decide at any moment to pray. When we decide, we turn our attention to God—we actively *intend* to communicate. At other times we may unconsciously communicate with God via our inmost thoughts, emotions, and intentions that underlie our actions. If we dedicate ourselves to seeking God with our whole heart, mind, and body, even when we aren't actively thinking about God, our whole approach toward life inclines us to hear and respond to God without even thinking about it. Just as we can respond unthinkingly to a "come hither" glance by an attractive person, so can we respond to our Mad Lover's subtle invitations to intimacy.

Paul's letter to the Romans tells us that the Holy Spirit even prays to the Father for us:

> Likewise the Spirit helps us in our weakness; for we do not know how to pray as we ought, but that very Spirit intercedes with sighs too deep for words. And God, who searches the heart, knows what is the mind of the Spirit, because the Spirit intercedes for the saints according to the will of God. (8:26–27)

God not only wants to speak loving words to us but even helps us communicate back, just like a loving parent helps a confused child to clarify what they really feel and to express it.

Prayer is a lot like water. The Hebrew Scriptures and the New Testament frequently talk about water. After all, the Hebrews lived in the midst of a desert. For them, water was a matter of life and death. When Jesus met the woman at the well, he talked about giving her "springs of living water" that never would go dry. In a vision, Ezekiel saw a life-giving stream that flowed from under the wall of the temple in Jerusalem. The Revelation to John speaks about the river of life flowing from the throne of God.

For water to flow, rain first must fall. When it hits the earth, one of two things happens. It either flows over the ground until it enters a stream, or it percolates underground until it becomes part of the aquifer. At some point the aquifer may surface so that its water flows out in a spring. This spring then brings water to any number of plants and animals along the watercourse that it feeds, just as the scriptural authors describe. If, however, all the rain flows overland into the creeks and streams, no water enters the aquifers and the springs dry up. All too many people throughout the world have discovered what happens to their water sources when the soil about them becomes impermeable either due to actions such as poor agricultural practices, planting trees (such as pines) that rapidly suck water out of the earth, or covering the soil up with asphalt and concrete. Aquifers require us to treat them with care, to ensure that the earth's surface can receive the rain and allow it to percolate deep within.

The Holy Spirit rains God's Word upon us, continually giving us the opportunity to receive refreshment, to recharge the aquifer of our spirit. As our spirit recharges, it surfaces and pours out of us, bringing life to all those around us. If our aquifer doesn't recharge, what flows out of us all too often brings illness and hurt.

How do intention, prayer, and water all flow together? When we take time to pray, we engage in an active intention to communicate with God. This gets our spring activated. Our active intention clears it of rocks, sticks, and other debris that would impede its flow. It gets us in touch with God. Our foundational intention to allow God to work in every moment of our lives, to make God manifest in the world through the way we live our lives, informs our approach to our everyday activities. We can *choose* to live in a way that cleanses our stream of pollutants and sediment so that it flows clearly and effectively, bringing health to all we touch. The *way* we approach our daily activities also prepares our soil to receive the Holy Spirit so that it can percolate deep within us and recharge the aquifer of our being. As Psalm 95:7b–8a says, "O that today you would listen to his voice! vvaDo not harden your heart."

Our task is to create an approach to life that enables springs of living water easily to flow from us. To do this, we may want to think in terms of water management. We need to clean our spring and to manage the recharge zone of our aquifer, our daily life. How do we do this?

Prayer and Water Management: Creating a Life Framework

Prayer Time: Cleaning the Spring

First, we need to work on getting our spring to flow clearly and freely. This means having a designated time for prayer. Most spiritual guides recommend at least twenty minutes per day, preferably first thing in the morning and, if possible, a similar time last thing at night.

At this point I can guess that you may be saying, "Great! How can I spend twenty minutes out of my day? In the morning I have to get the kids off to school or me off to work. By the time night comes, I just fall asleep." Well, we never said that this would be easy! If you want to run a marathon, lose weight, or learn to speak Spanish, it requires effort, time, and commitment. In the same manner, if you want to learn to pray, you have to decide whether or not this is worth it to you. Growing spiritually means going into training. It means passing "through the eye of a needle." So decide now whether or not you want to make the commitment.

That said, there are no rules in all this. If twenty minutes looks impossible right now, try five minutes or ten. Can you get up five minutes earlier? Or if first thing in the morning truly is impossible, what about lunchtime?

Keep two key things in mind. First, it's most helpful if you can start off your day focusing on the Lord, getting in touch. This helps you remember your foundational intention to live in a way that enables you to live a prayer. The time in the evening helps you remember, after a day of distractions and fumbles, what your life is all about. This way, when you get up in the morning, you already have a bit of a head start on remembering what you're trying to do. You're already a bit more in touch. Morning and evening prayer, even if brief, bookend your day. This is the principle. How you implement it is up to you.

Second, our lives often aren't ideal. We face demanding schedules and obligations that make it difficult for us to arrange our day as we would like. So *do the best you can and let God do the rest*. Start small, take little steps. If a particular time for prayer doesn't work, try another. If need be, take the spiritual equivalent of power naps—keep in mind your intention to pray when the opportunity presents itself and grab the moment when it comes. Ask the Holy Spirit to guide you in all this. You can be assured that God will honor your desire and will help you grow despite all of the challenges you face. God wants to be close to you even more than you want to be close to God. So you can trust that God will be with you and guide you even when you don't know it.

Once you have a time to pray, how do you go about doing it? There are about as many ways to pray as there are people, and about as many books on prayer. I've included a few of the latter at the end of this book. These are books I've found particularly helpful. Many other people have found them useful too. That said, here a few thoughts to help you get started in prayer, if you haven't already.

As I said earlier, first and foremost, prayer consists of communication with God. So when you decide to have your prayer time, remind yourself about what you are doing. Tell yourself that you have dedicated this time to getting in touch with God. Remind yourself that you want your life to be one whereby you manifest God to the world and see God everywhere, that you want to love God with your whole mind, body, and spirit. In other words, remember why you're there.

Sit in a comfortable chair, preferably one with a straight back. With your feet flat on the floor, sit up straight. You may need a cushion behind your back to help you do this in an alert, but relaxed, way. If your body is alert, so will your spirit be.

If your mind is racing on with all sorts of concerns, you might find that this is a good time to read some scripture or a spiritual book. This might help you focus. Although this itself need not be prayer (it actually could become a distraction), it can be an effective way to get your mind off of the day's events and reorient it to God.

If we want to communicate with God, we need to devote our attention to that intention. However, our mind tends to get in our way, rattling on and distracting us. Sometimes we may get obsessed about something and find it difficult to concentrate on anything else. So quiet prayer requires some means for dealing with our thoughts.

I find, as many do, that relaxing breaths provide a very effective means of centering myself, of focusing myself on my intention of communicating with God. Sit up straight and focus all your attention on how the breath feels as it goes in and out of your nose. What sensations do you notice? Try breathing in slowly through your nose for a count of say four to six, and then exhale through barely parted lips for four to six counts. Do this several times and allow your body to relax.

If thoughts pop into your mind (as they always do), just notice that they are there without thinking about them and then return your attention to your breath. *Don't fight the thoughts—* they are part of who you are. Just acknowledge their presence and then go back to paying attention to your breath. If you try to get rid of them, you will divert your attention to that effort instead of just being present to God.

Having relaxed, now remember your intention to be open to God and allow God to speak to you in silence. Often the deepest moments of communication with people we care about consist of those times we sit quietly with one another, saying nothing. Do the same with God. If you find your mind starting to intrude, go back to noticing your breath. When and if your mind calms down, just sit quietly, thinking nothing. Allow the silence itself to speak to you. Let it permeate you. The first lesson of this program provides a more detailed description of this process for you.

Centering prayer takes a similar approach. Instead of focusing on the breath, centering prayer asks you to choose a "sacred word" such as "peace," "Jesus," or "Spirit" as your focal point. You then repeat the word slowly in your mind. When you become aware that your thoughts have distracted you, calmly and gently return your attention to the sacred word. Use your breath and a sacred word to occupy our mind.

Toward the end of your prayer time, voice your concerns to God. Speak to God like you would to your best friend, knowing that your Friend can handle your anxiety, anger, and sadness, as well as share your joy. Pray for people who need help, for your needs and those of your loved ones, and for the great needs of the world.

When it is time to close, thank God for this time and ask the Holy Spirit to open your mind and heart as you proceed with the rest of your day (or your sleep).

There is no such thing as good or bad prayer. There's just prayer. Sitting down and trying to pray, however "spiritual" or not it feels, speaks strongly of your desire to come closer to God. Remember, it's the Holy Spirit ultimately who will pray in and for you. Just be open to whatever happens and trust the Spirit to do what needs to be done. Just show up and leave the rest in God's hands.

Making Our Soil Permeable

If we hope to receive the Holy Spirit's recharging water during our waking hours, we need to create a framework for our lives that helps us be open to its working. We need to create a permeable surface. Traditionally this has involved scripture reading, reading spiritual books, service, fasting, and almsgiving. Once again, don't give up because it sounds like a long list of things to do. Just be aware of them and see how you might start incorporating them into your life bit by bit.

Without a doubt, reading the Bible needs to be an integral part of our life. This may mean five minutes a day or more when you get a chance. It's not a matter of reading a lot at a time, but reading it with an open heart. It helps both to know what the Bible says in a factual sort of way and to know what the Bible is speaking to you at this point in time. You will find that the same Bible passage will hit you differently at different points in your life.

Many people find *lectio divina*, a Benedictine way of reading the Bible, a deeply satisfying form of contemplative prayer. Choose a Bible passage and read it *slowly* aloud. Then read it aloud again very slowly, perhaps just a couple of words at a time. You may find that a small phrase or word will catch your attention or move you in some way. Sit with those words, and reflect on them. What do they speak to you? How do they move you? What do they say about you? about God? about your relationship with God? Lastly, without thinking about them, allow these words to roll around in your heart and mind. Repeat them inwardly and absorb them into your being. You can take these words with you during your day, repeating them during the day and remembering them. They can nourish you and sustain you if you allow them to accompany you.

We need others to guide us. God doesn't intend us to journey alone. After all, we rely on our elders for advice, whether it be spiritual or financial. So read spiritual books and gain from the wisdom they have to offer. Similarly, seek people with whom you can share your spiritual life. Prayer groups and Bible studies can serve this function. So can finding a spiritually mature person with whom you can pray and discuss your life with God. You might consider finding a spiritual director who can help you discern the Holy Spirit's guidance in your life and to act on it.

Seek out a way or ways you can express your faith in the world. This might mean setting up chairs at a prayer meeting, taking lunches to shut-ins, visiting someone who is sick, or just trying to speak a kind word to someone each day. The more we give to others because we love God, the more we enable God to reach into our own hearts and expand them. It makes the soil of our lives more able to absorb the water of the Spirit. Similarly, sharing one's resources, whether one's abilities, time, or money, to help others (almsgiving) is an important way to stretch our hearts and open them to others and to God.

Finally, let's consider fasting. Typically this has involved curtailing food consumption for one meal, a day, or longer. We do this not to beat ourselves into submission, but rather to help us wake up. Eating less, for instance, with the intention of opening our hearts to God is a way of putting God ahead of something that has taken too much importance in our lives. Our physical hunger reminds us of our hunger for God. It reminds us of our fundamental intention.

So, in essence, fasting consists of identifying those things in our lives that rule our behavior: sex, texting, food, money, control, or an innumerable number of other things. As you pray, ask

God to show you one thing that you feel you can't do without and that distracts you from being open to God's love. You may feel the need, for instance, to check social media frequently "just in case." This is an addiction that controls your behavior. So consider a social media fast for an hour, morning, or day. Trust in God to give you the strength to do without it and to open you to the Spirit's presence. Do this periodically, perhaps once a week, and you will experience great freedom. When you come to the point that you can choose when and if you will check in on social media, then ask God to show you your next area where you need to be freed.

Going Forward

Work patiently and gently to get your prayer time and prayer life going. Fit in scripture reading, spiritual reading, service, and fasting and almsgiving as best you can, incorporating them into your life more fully over time. We are leaving these aspects of growing spiritually up to you. They will provide a context and fuel to help you move forward on our work together. Feel free to use the resources of your church or faith community, if you have one, to help you in these things. Or seek a faith community that can help you grow in these areas.

Over the next weeks we will be working on changing our approach to our daily lives so that we can learn to encounter God wherever we are, in whatever we are doing. We will incarnate our fundamental intention in the way we go about our lives. To do this, we will seek God where God may be found—in the work of God's hands. We will turn to the rest of creation to teach us lessons that we can take into our distracted everyday lives. Practicing those lessons every day will form us and make us more pliable in God's hands. We then will be more capable of learning from the rest of creation. The world through which the Holy Spirit moves will be our monastery, our teacher.

Resources on Prayer

Bloom, Anthony. *Beginning to Pray*. New York: Paulist Press, 1970.

Brother Lawrence. *The Practice of the Presence of God*. Old Tappan, NJ: Spire Books, 1958.

Centering prayer and *lectio divina* brochures downloadable from Contemplative Outreach: http://www.contemplative outreach.org/category/category/workshops.

de Mello, Anthony. *Sadhanna: A Way to God: Christian Exercises in Eastern Form*. New York: Doubleday, 1984.

_____. *The Song of the Bird*. New York: Doubleday, 1982.

de Waal, Esther. *Living with Contradiction: An Introduction to Benedictine Spirituality*. Harrisburg, PA: Morehouse Publishing, 1998.

Fischer, Kathleen. *Loving Creation: Christian Spirituality, Earth-Centered and Just*. Mahwah, NJ: Paulist Press, 2009.

Frenette, David. "Present to Presence: The Contemplative Practice of Attention/Intention." *Sewanee Theological Review* 53, no. 3 (2010): 274–84.

Merton, Thomas. *A Book of Hours*. Edited by Kathleen Deignan. Notre Dame, IN: Sorin Books, 2007.

_____. *New Seeds of Contemplation*. New York: New Directions, 1961.

Pennington, M. Basil. *Centering Prayer: Renewing an Ancient Christian Prayer Form*. New York: Doubleday, 1982.

Steindl-Rast, David. *Gratefulness: The Heart of Prayer: An Approach to Life in Fullness*. New York: Paulist Press, 1984.

_____. *A Listening Heart: The Spirituality of Sacred Sensuousness*. New York: Crossroads, 1999.